THE GREAT AMERICAN

FARM TRACTOR

THE GREAT AMERICAN FARM TRACTOR

C. H. WENDEL

Published by Longmeadow Press, 201 High Ridge Road, Stamford, CT 06904.

Longmeadow Press and the colophon are registered trademarks.

ISBN 0-681-00397-9

Printed in China

First Longmeadow Press Edition

0 9 8 7 6 5 4 3 2 1

PAGE 1:
The 1938 Graham-Bradley 32 hp was sold by Sears Roebuck & Company.

PAGE 2:
The John Deere Model 4440 with a row-crop cultivator works a cornfield in Iowa.

BELOW:
The Caterpillar D7, powered by a six-cylinder diesel engine, was introduced in the late 1930s.

CONTENTS

Introduction

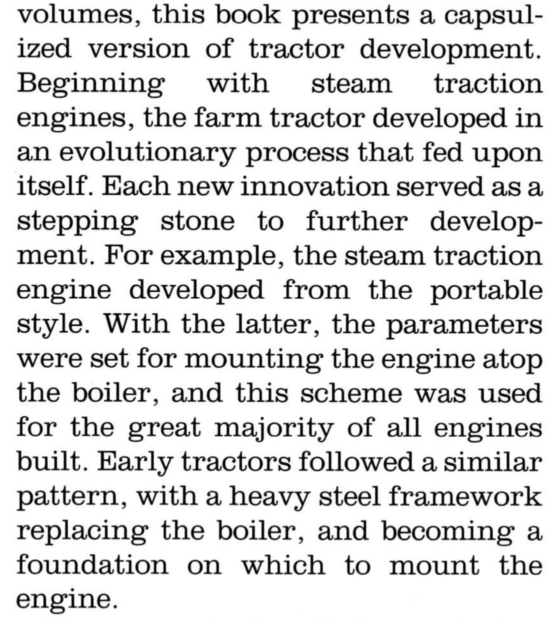

The development of the American farm tractor is the very essence of mechanized agriculture. Even though the reaper mechanized the cutting of grain, and although the thresher mechanized the harvest, the tractor became the quintessential component of change. This book traces the development of the farm tractor, from the heavy and cumbersome steam traction engines of the nineteenth century to today's modern farm tractors.

Even though the complete history of the farm tractor could require many volumes, this book presents a capsulized version of tractor development. Beginning with steam traction engines, the farm tractor developed in an evolutionary process that fed upon itself. Each new innovation served as a stepping stone to further development. For example, the steam traction engine developed from the portable style. With the latter, the parameters were set for mounting the engine atop the boiler, and this scheme was used for the great majority of all engines built. Early tractors followed a similar pattern, with a heavy steel framework replacing the boiler, and becoming a foundation on which to mount the engine.

BELOW:
A lineup of pre-1940 machines intrigues vintage tractor buffs at the annual Midwest Old Threshers' Reunion.

The concept of unit frame design began about 1912, and has become the universally accepted method of tractor frame design. Even though some companies steadfastly held to the earlier heavyweight designs, virtually all of them succumbed to the unit frame design by the early 1930s.

International Harvester Company developed the Farmall row-crop tractor in the 1920s. Subsequently, all row-crop tractor design would follow the standard set by International Harvester. Although many variants have been built, the basic row-crop design remains unchanged even to the present time. Four-wheel-drive designs also began emerging in the 1920s. In this instance, inventive ideas were ahead of the available technology. Not until the 1950s would four-wheel-drive tractors attain any significance, and not until the 1960s did they achieve important status within the industry.

Crawler tractors have enjoyed a special status within mechanized agriculture. A few companies specialized in crawler tractors, while others included them as part of their overall equipment line. Cleveland Tractor Company was one of the first to promote the crawler as an all-purpose farm tractor. Their Cletrac models were fitted with cultivators and other equipment during the 1920s and gained considerable popularity.

There is no doubt that much of today's farm tractor development has been borrowed from other industries. For example, tractor engines were initially an adaptation of early stationary engines. Meanwhile, automobile and truck development continued, and companies like Buda at Harvey, Illinois, promoted their lightweight, high-speed designs for tractor duty. Eventually, the heavy, slow-speed engines would be replaced with high-speed engines using four, six, and even eight cylinders.

Early tractor designers favored kerosene for tractor fuel. By the 1930s kerosene fell into disfavor, with distillate enjoying a brief life. The latter could well be described as something between gasoline and kerosene. By the 1950s, gasoline engines were by far the most popular style, but the diesel engine was quickly rising to the top. It had been developed for tractor use already in the 1930s and made slow, quiet progress into the 1950s. Eventually the diesel engine gained favor, with the result that the vast majority of farm tractors are now equipped with diesel engines.

Transmissions and drive trains have seen similar development. From one or two forward speeds, farm tractors are now built with power shift transmissions that permit the operator to shift on-the-go, with no clutching or stopping.

These are but some of the significant innovations, detailed herein, that have made the American farm tractor what it is today. Attending shows and collecting vintage tractors are becoming ever more popular as a means to glimpse a tangible part of an agrarian past, and to image how tractor development affected farming practices – and vice versa. The evolving designs of the American farm tractor mirror the evolution of the collective minds of engineers, inventors, entrepreneurs, farmers and others who have played a significant part in American agricultural history.

LEFT:
A detail of the colorful 1948 Case LA, a model that was popular from 1940 to 1955.

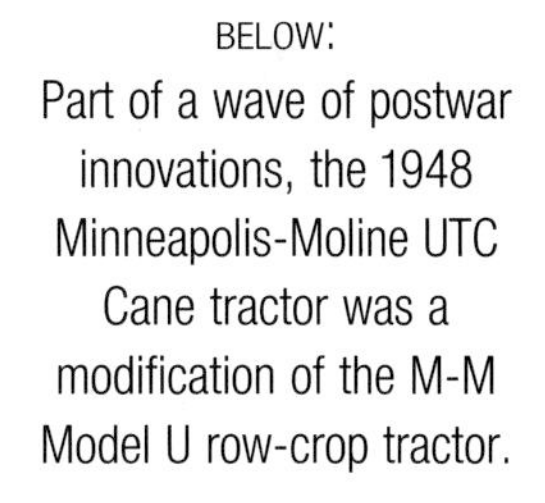

BELOW:
Part of a wave of postwar innovations, the 1948 Minneapolis-Moline UTC Cane tractor was a modification of the M-M Model U row-crop tractor.

CHAPTER 1: Beginnings to 1910

PAGES 8-9:
Farmers in upstate New York display their ox-drawn reaper, circa 1900.

BELOW:
The 1886 Watertown traction engine.

OPPOSITE TOP:
The 1880s Buffalo Pitts portable engine was powered by coal or wood.

OPPOSITE BOTTOM:
People traveled for miles to see this innovative, labor-saving McCormick harvester and wire binder of 1876.

ONLY IN RECENT years has the farm tractor gained recognition for its role in changing the American lifestyle. But the tractor was not the beginning of mechanized agriculture. It was but a step in a process that had begun in reality during the 1830s, and in the minds of inventors long before that. The reaper was the first major farm equipment development. Although its beginnings can be traced with accuracy to 1831, the reaper did not gain wide acceptance for another 20 years. The grain thresher was developed about the same time, and it too, waited two decades for widespread acceptance. Meanwhile, America remained a largely agrarian country, with farming of any kind being highly labor-intensive.

Paralleling the development of the reaper, the thresher, and a few other farm implements was the birth of the steam locomotive. It too, came along in the 1830s, and within 20 years it attained a significant degree of development. By 1850, fertile minds were at work on using the power of steam to operate a grain thresher. These ideas reached only moderate success until about 1870, when the first practical and successful portable steam engines were marketed commercially. However, during the 1850-1870 period, a few portable engines were built and sold, but the numbers were few, the price was high, and farmer acceptance was only lukewarm. The most significant development of the period was the portable engine built by J. I. Case at Racine, Wisconsin. It was first built in 1869, and proved to be the foundation for a product line which endures to the present time.

In order to better understand the dynamics of the time, it is important to look at the mindset of the average

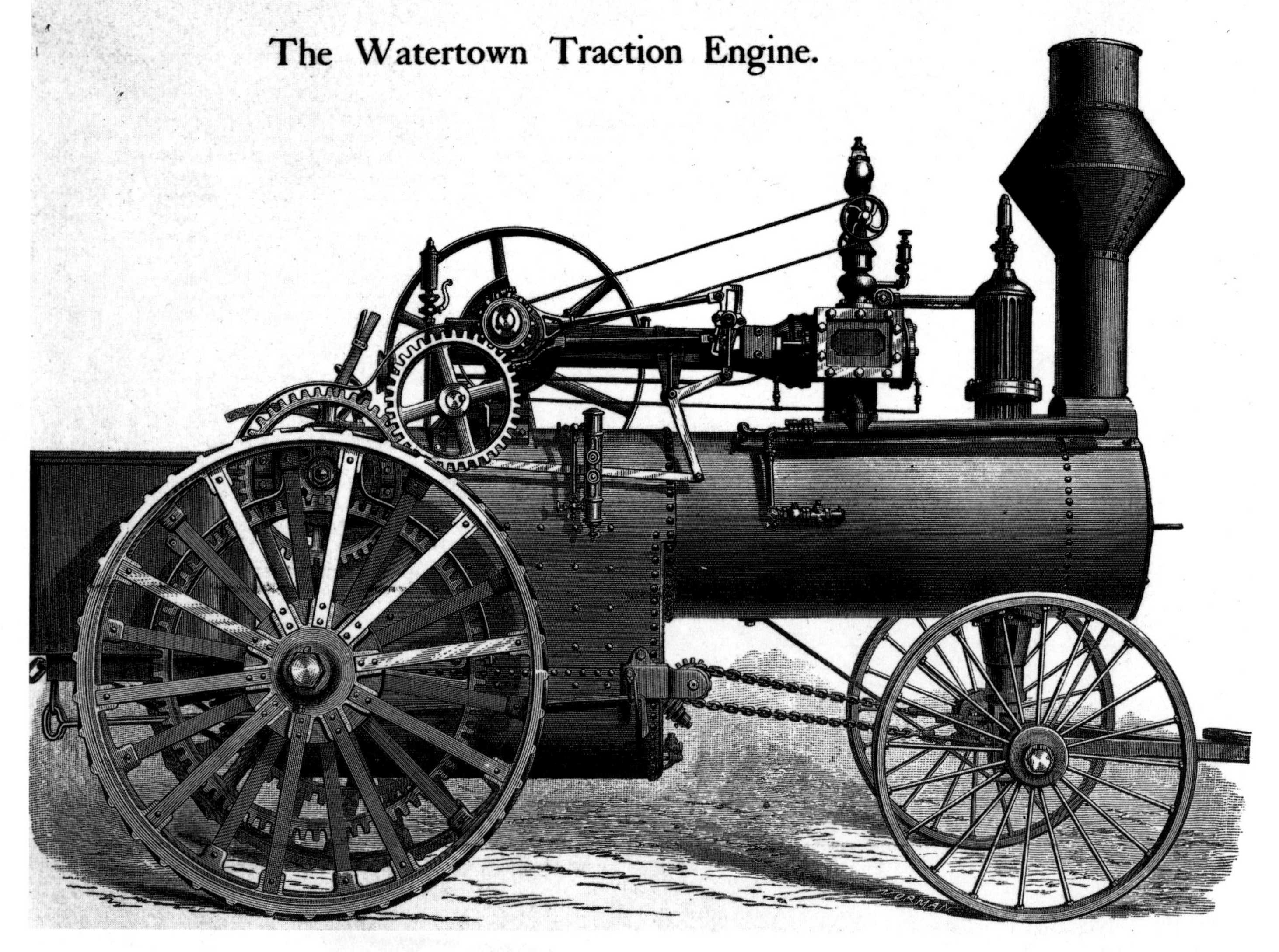

farmer of the 1850s. For most, strict religious training was a given fact. Living by the sweat of one's brow was part and parcel of American farm life. After preparing the soil and planting the seed, the rest was up to a stern and mighty Creator. If a good crop was harvested, then it came only from a gracious and beneficient God. If, on the other hand, the crop was damaged or destroyed by flood, hail or pestilence, then again, this was God's will. The negativistic attitudes of many farmers to horse-powered machines greatly diminished their interest in the field. Adding the new dynamic of steam power was virtually an anathema. Until attitudes changed, any sort of "power equipment" gained little public interest. For many farmers, the adage that "This is the way we've always done it" was quite sufficient for their needs.

The majority of Americans lived in agricultural areas until the 1920s. In his book, *Machines, Men and Morality*, Robert Sobel notes that "America seemed a utopia for farmers" of the 1850s. Because farming methods of

ABOVE:
Barzee & Silver's combined harvester of 1880 was pulled by 24 horses. Early farm machinery did not replace, but worked in conjunction with, horses and oxen, supplying the extra efficiency needed at harvest time.

the 1850s were so labor-intensive, and since there was a scarcity of farm labor to harvest the crops, many farmers abandoned the notion of taking their chances on whatever the soil returned. Farming practices became more intensive, and a new publishing industry emerged, that of the farm press. Meanwhile, as crop production increased, the demand for farm labor was insatiable. Driven by the need for relief, agriculture took a new look at mechanization.

Another major obstacle to the development of farm power and farm equipment generally was the lack of technology to build the machines that existed in the minds of inventors. United States Patents for 1837 totaled 435, of which only a small portion were for farm machines. Nearly 2,200 applications were filed in 1850 alone, and a substantial number related to farm implements, appliances and other items related to America's agrarian economy. Twenty years later, in 1870, over 19,000 patent applications were filed, and in 1909 the total number of applications was 65,839. From these figures alone the evolution of American invention can be put in perspective; technology was at least beginning to catch up to inventors' dreams.

The technology of early farm equipment was confined primarily to the local blacksmith. From his shop came crude plows, harrows and various hand tools. Literally thousands of minds were simultaneously engaged in developing the grain thresher, for example. Small factories sprang up across the country, and many of these were little more than glorified blacksmith shops. Eventually, the best features of one machine would be found on another. Perhaps the form would be different, perhaps the appearance would vary, but in an evolutionary process, all the salient features came together to form an efficient and reliable machine. The same process held true for the development of the American farm tractor. It didn't spring from dormant and unseasoned minds overnight; it developed in staircase fashion, with new innovations being stacked above previous designs. The process continues.

Manufacturing technologies and machine tools became highly developed by the 1880s. The concept of interchangeability of parts also came into its own during this time. As machines became more complicated, it was imperative that replacement parts fit exactly like the originals. This point is more clearly made in relation to the Appleby twine knotter. This rather complicated mechanism used a number of parts made to very close tolerances, so replacement parts had to fit exactly into place. By 1880 most manufacturers were quite capable of manufacturing interchangeable parts, machining them either to a gauge or to a micrometer. The development of the American machine tool industry was thus tied hand-in-hand to the development of all machinery in general, and machine tool development was also an essential component of farm equipment manufacturing.

Most early farm equipment was built in a setting close to its market. Until the coming of the railroad and other means of public transportation, rural communities were virtual entities unto themselves. There was no reliable mail service, and the mass media of our time could hardly have been imagined. These factors all combined to thwart the concept of centralized manufacturing and regional distribution centers which we now accept as standard practice. Until the development of sales methods and a transportation system, centralized manufacturing was not to achieve any great success.

Successful selling requires first that the customer become convinced of the need for a certain product. Beginning in earnest by the 1870s, farmers were encouraged to request annual catalogs from newly emerging manufacturers. Thus began a new era in salesmanship, that of direct advertising through catalogs, circulars and postcards. The emerging farm press also carried advertising. Although many farm magazines were of regional interest, they brought the message to thousands of farmers who had previously been unapproachable.

A look at farm machinery catalogs of the period following 1870 provides a look at farm equipment development over the years, and also provides an insight into sales methods of the time. Many machinery catalogs featured beautiful lithographed covers. Inside were wood engravings of a quality to rival anything in the history of printing. The written commentaries were often enhanced with testimonial letters from satisfied users.

BELOW:
Early farm machinery catalogs, like this later Avery catalog from 1918, featured appealing artwork and stylish graphics. A vital ingredient in a growing inventory of early sales methods, these vintage catalogs have today become collector's items.

Fairs and expositions provided another avenue of salesmanship. By 1880 county fairs had attained great popularity, becoming a major event of the year. The climax was the state fair, to those who were fortunate enough to attend. Major companies expended great sums of money in shipping their line of equipment to the fairs, along with sending along their best territory men to convince farmers of the need to buy. Special catalogs and circulars were provided to attendees.

Another sales approach was the ordinary penny postcard. These were usually lithographed, some were embossed, and many were die cut to a special design. Some even carried a small printed calendar on the back. The almanac was another favorite sales tool. International Harvester issued its almanac for many years, as an example.

Once the obstacles to farm mechanization – farmer resistance, lack of technology and of centralized transportation systems – began to topple, the stage was set for power farming to develop. As manufacturing technologies, sales techniques and distribution systems improved, the pieces were in place for the development of the American farm tractor to proceed apace.

American farm tractor development can readily be traced to two distinct roots: the development of the portable steam engine and the gasoline engine. The portable steam engine evolved into the steam traction engine by the 1880s. Early traction engines were primarily intended to propel themselves from place to place, while perhaps pulling the grain thresher or some other machine behind. Many of the early traction engines used horses to steer the front axle. Power applied to the traction wheels eliminated the load on the horses, and that was the chief advantage.

Steering mechanisms weren't developed until about 1880; likewise, the differential gear came into use about the same time. Steering mechanisms of this time usually consisted of a stiff front bolster as used on a wagon. Heavy chains were attached to the axle and terminated on a large steering drum. The drum was turned by a worm gear under the control of the engineer. So-called "auto steering,"

BELOW:
An early Advance-Rumely steam engine. In 1911 Rumely bought the Advance Thresher Company and Gaar-Scott, a company dating back to 1870.

LEFT:
The Paxton traction engine of 1884 was produced by the Kingsland & Ferguson Manufacturing Company.

using kingpins and tie rods connected to a steering gear, was a development of the automotive industry. During the 1880s and into the 1890s, steam power continued to develop, reaching its peak about 1910. As stream traction engines developed, so did manufacturing methods and technologies. Large areas were being plowed for the first time, using the steam engine. Despite its steady and reliable power, the steam engine had numerous disadvantages. Sparks from the smokestack were likely to ignite a strawstack or a barn. A substantial number of threshers, strawstacks and barns were lost this way. The steam engine required a capable engineer. Low water was likely to cause an explosion. Indeed, a fairly large number of engines did explode, due to either low water or improper maintenance. Oftentimes this happened with a loss of life, or at least with dreadful injuries.

Plowing and other traction work required several men to accomplish. There was an engineer and a fireman on the engine. Steam plows were usually fitted with individual beams that had to be raised and lowered one at a time by the plow tender. The support crew included a water hauler and a coal hauler. In many instances, a cook was also required to feed the crew three big hearty meals a day. Farmers wanted something better, and inventive efforts turned toward the gasoline tractor.

Early Development of the Gas Tractor

In 1876 N. A. Otto of Germany developed the "Otto Silent," which was the first successful four-cycle gas engine. Parenthetically, the term "gas engine," which we use freely today, originally denoted an engine using natural, producer, or some other form of gaseous vapor for fuel. The "gasoline engine" was an engine that used liquid fuel. Otto began manufacturing the "Silent" at Philadelphia in 1880. From these efforts came today's American engine industry.

John Charter at Sterling, Illinois, built a gasoline engine in 1882. His first engine patent was issued in 1875, and numerous patents were issued to Charter in the following years. His son, James A. Charter, went to Beloit, Wisconsin, in 1893 as a designer for Fairbanks, Morse & Company. His designs characterized the Fairbanks-Morse engines for decades to come.

ABOVE:
A threshing crew in Minnesota around the turn of the century employs the massive Advance strawburning engine and a similarly proportioned thresher. The Advance Thresher Company of Battle Creek, Michigan, began operations in 1881.

The success of the Charter engines at Sterling led John Charter to mount one of his engines on a steam engine chassis in 1889. Even though this was a big, clumsy machine, it nevertheless was probably the first successful American farm tractor. Charter operated this engine on a threshing machine in the Dakotas during the harvest season, but for reasons obscured by time, the Charter gasoline traction engine never achieved commercial success. In fact, so far as is known, Charter Gas Engine Company never entered the gas tractor business. Shortly after, the Otto Gas Engine Company built a similar design, mounting one of their big, stationary engines on a steam engine chassis. Like Charter, the Otto never saw commercial success.

One of the first companies organized solely for the production of gasoline tractors was the Waterloo Gasoline Traction Engine Company at Waterloo, Iowa, in 1893. John Froehlich built his first gasoline tractor in the tiny northeastern Iowa village of Froehlich during 1892. The success of this first venture prompted Froehlich to apply for a patent in 1893. During 1895, he was issued U.S. Patent No. 550,266 for his design. During 1893 Froelich moved to Waterloo, establishing a company there, and concentrating his efforts on building a better tractor. Despite his work, the experiments did not yield a commercially successful tractor at the start. Thus, other investors turned to the gasoline engine business to support the inventive work on tractors. It appears that Froehlich was unhappy with the decision of his partners and left the company shortly thereafter. Froehlich appeared later at St. Paul, Minnesota. He was actively engaged in the development of the Hackney tractor which emerged from the Hackney Mfg. Company in 1911. Despite its sound design, the Hackney disappeared from the scene in 1918.

After its inception, the Waterloo Gasoline Traction Engine Company experimented for a couple of fruitless years, then reorganized simply as the Waterloo Gasoline Engine Company. Concentrating its efforts solely on gasoline engines, the firm became eminently successful in its field. Little is known of the company's tractor efforts during the following 20 years. While it is certain that tractor experiments had resumed in earnest by 1909, these developments remained secondary to the gasoline engine business.

Louis W. Witry became the Chief Engineer for the Waterloo Gasoline

Engine Company in the early 1900s, perhaps even earlier. His designs resulted in the famous Waterloo Boy tractor introduced in 1914. It was a lightweight design, compared to most of its peers, and was an overnight success. This impressive design caught the attention of Deere & Company. On March 18, 1918, Deere purchased the Waterloo Gasoline Engine Company for $2,100,000.

In 1901 Hart-Parr Company began building "tractors" at Charles City, Iowa. This company was the first one devoted exclusively to the farm tractor business, and in many respects was the founder of the American farm tractor industry. The company also adopted the term "tractor" in its advertising. This was much simpler than the cumbersome term, "gasoline traction engine." The term "tractor" originated at the time of Shakespeare, but Hart-Parr was apparently the first to apply it to their new invention.

The Hart-Parr used an engine built specifically for the purpose. Prior to the Hart-Parr most manufacturing efforts attempted to incorporate a stationary engine design with a custom-built chassis. Hart-Parr's innovation was a major advance in tractor design. Even though the weight-to-horsepower ratio of these early engines was far higher than today, it was a significant improvement over the extra, and unneeded, cast iron of a stationary engine adaptation.

Hart-Parr designs were innovative in numerous ways, most notably in the use of cut steel gears. Far more strength could be obtained from steel gears than from those of cast iron, and this with less weight. Beginning in 1903 the Hart-Parr used an oil coolant. It eliminated the worries about winter freeze-up, and permitted the higher cylinder temperatures required for burning kerosene and similar low-grade fuels. Above all, the Hart-Parr design was reliable, and this was a major selling point. In fact, the 30-60 tractor introduced in 1907 soon took the name of "Old Reliable." Thus rated,

BELOW:
The Gaar-Scott Company of Richmond, Indiana, produced the gas-powered Tigerpull tractor. A long-time manufacturer of steam engines, threshers and other farm machinery, Gaar-Scott began producing gasoline tractors in 1911, three decades after N.A. Otto built the first successful gas engine.

ABOVE:
The 1908 Capital gasoline traction engine was an early entrant in the field, produced by C.H.A. Dissinger & Bro. Company, Inc., of Lancaster, Pennsylvania.

BELOW:
An early Case steam tractor is a featured attraction at the annual Ozarks Steam Engine Festival in Republic, Missouri.

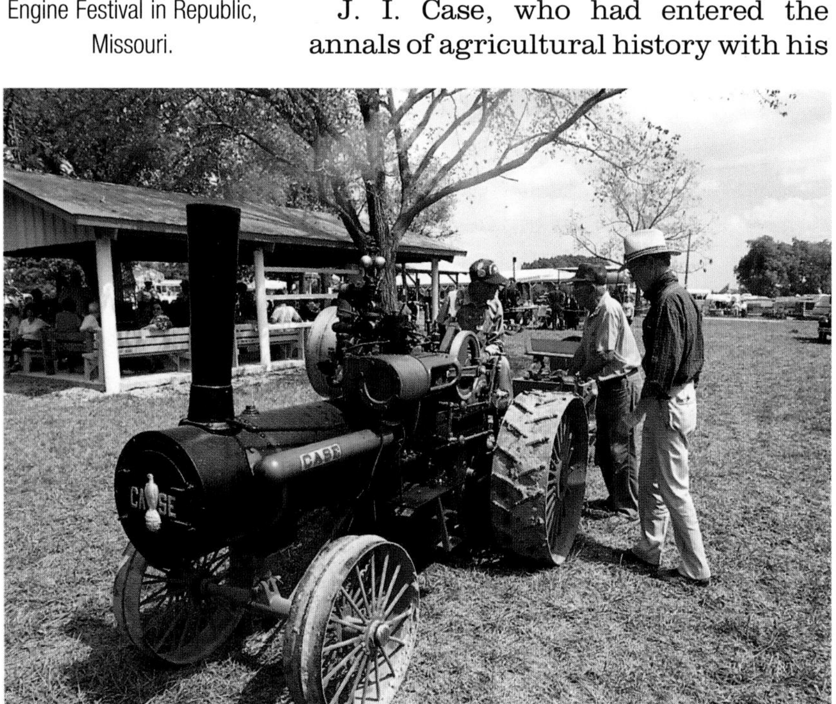

the first number indicates drawbar horsepower, and the second number is the belt horsepower. It was built until 1918. However, by that time tractor designs were rapidly changing, and the market for large, heavyweight tractors like "Old Reliable" began to disappear. Farmers were clamoring for a small, lightweight tractor suitable for the average 160-acre Midwestern farm. Hart-Parr answered that year with their New Hart-Parr. It was a lightweight design built in several sizes until the company merged with other firms to form the Oliver Farm Equipment Company in 1929.

J. I. Case, who had entered the annals of agricultural history with his grain thresher of 1842 and the Case portable steam engine of 1869, ventured into the gasoline tractor business with the "Paterson" tractor in 1892. The lack of satisfactory carburetion and ignition led to the Paterson's demise, and the J. I. Case Threshing Machine Company would not re-enter the gasoline tractor business for nearly 20 years. When the company once again entered the tractor business, it did so in a very cautious manner. Full production of gas tractors commenced only after success was assured.

At this point carburetors were not yet developed to any degree, and gasoline engine ignition was unreliable at its best. In fact, many engine designers of the 1890s considered electric ignition to be quite out of the question; their preferred favorite was hot tube ignition. The latter was quite unsatisfactory for a tractor, and there were as yet no reliable batteries or ignition dynamos; once again ideas were running ahead of technology.

In lieu of carburetors, the early Charter gasoline engines used a crude form of fuel injection which worked creditably well. Other inventors concentrated on various forms of vaporizing devices, but none of them worked in a reliable fashion. Many of the carburetor developments subsequently used were previously developed for automotive use, yet another aspect of the overall development of the American farm tractor. By the early 1900s the Kingston, the Holley, and other carburetors appeared. Companies sprang up that specialized in carburetors and ignition devices. Entire new industries developed that remain to this day.

A great many of the early tractor builders had originally begun as grain thresher manufacturers. Grain threshers required considerable power, and the steam engine was a logical candidate to provide it. Initially, the gasoline tractor was met with disdain by the so-called "old-line" thresher builders. In fact, when Hart-Parr ran their first advertisement in a 1902 issue of *American Threshermen*

Magazine, several of the steam engine builders threatened to pull all their advertising from this journal if it continued to accept Hart-Parr advertising. Hart-Parr advertising continued, sales grew, and soon after there were more tractor advertisements. Within 10 years the advertising for steam engines had largely been replaced with ads for gas tractors of all sizes, shapes and descriptions.

Of all tractors to be announced in the first decade of the twentieth century, none gained the longstanding reputation of the Rumely OilPull. Advance-Rumely Thresher Company would merge with Allis-Chalmers in 1931. Although the venerable OilPull hasn't been built in over 60 years, it remains as one of the most popular tractors.

The OilPull had a distinctive appearance with its very heavy framework and a large, square, box-type radiator. Within the box were separate sections or cells, and these carried the oil coolant. The radiator had an open bottom to permit free upward circulation of air. The engine exhaust was piped to a point above the radiator sections and terminated in nozzles pointing upward. With this system the engine exhaust provided an induced draft, carrying cool air upward over the radiator sections. The harder the engine worked, the heavier the draft, and consequently the volume of cooling air increased as well. On light loads, very little air passed over the sections. This created a virtually automatic cooling system with very accurate temperature regulation.

A salient feature of the OilPull was its high compression engine design. Another feature was the oil coolant, used instead of water. By using oil, the cylinder jacket temperature could be raised somewhat, and this, combined with the high compression engine, permitted the OilPull to burn kerosene and other low-grade fuels. In fact, every OilPull was "guaranteed to burn any fuel at any speed." At the time kerosene was quite inexpensive, and was widely used in tractor engines. However, to minimize preignition, it was necessary to inject water into the air-fuel mixture; the OilPull consumed about as much water as kerosene over the day's run.

Massively built, the OilPull quickly gained a reputation in the tractor industry. When this tractor emerged in 1910, the farm tractor business was dominated by big power, suitable for threshing, sawmills and plowing, but totally unsuited to the average quarter-section farm. Rumely expanded the series to include sizes from the big 30-60 down to a small 12-20 size better suited to the small farm. Yet, the days of the big tractor were numbered; farmers wanted small, lightweight tractors that could be used on the farm everyday. Thus, the OilPull and its peers would succumb to the evolutionary process that has

ABOVE:
A Rumely OilPull 20-23 in the field. The popular and powerful OilPull series emerged in 1910 and featured heavyweight designs.

ABOVE:
A 20-ton tractor, built in 1900 by the Best Manufacturing Company.

BELOW:
The Aultman Company's 1898 Star engine.

yielded today's great American farm tractor.

Another major player in the farm tractor business was Aultman & Taylor at Mansfield, Ohio. This company went back to 1867 as a grain thresher builder. Subsequently, A & T began building steam traction engines. In 1910 they began building gas tractors. The 30-60 model was characterized by huge 90-inch drivewheels and a big four-cylinder engine. It weighed on the order of 25,000 pounds!

At this point, it is significant to note that the matter of engine design was largely undecided in the period up to 1930. Virtually every cylinder configuration was used. Some tractors used a single-cylinder engine, but the two-cylinder style was the most popular for some years. A few used three-cylinder engines, and a fair number used four-cylinder motors. Very few tractors built prior to 1930 used a six-cylinder engine. Most tractor designers of the period held high speed automotive designs in disdain; the long-stroke, slow speed engine was preferred. Small, lightweight engine designs were brought to the forefront with the introduction of the Fordson tractor in 1917. Despite the popularity of the Fordson, and despite the advantages of the lightweight design, many tractor builders were slow to make the change, and others steadfastly refused. Those who persisted in old design methods succumbed to farmer preference for small tractors.

The 1910-1912 period can be considered to mark the real beginnings of the farm tractor. Granted, Hart-Parr had already built up a substantial business by this time, and International Harvester was making major noises with its developing tractor line. A few others were on the market, but most of the major farm equipment builders, particularly thresher manufacturers, entered the market in the 1910-1912 period. One of the major players in the business was the Avery Company at Peoria, Illinois.

Avery Company had a long history going back to the 1870s. Initially the company made corn planters and other farm equipment. During the 1880s the company began building threshing machines, and in 1891 they began making steam traction engines. Twenty years later, in 1911, the company started marketing their Avery tractor. From the initial model came a wide range of sizes. Small farms or large ranches could feasibly be graced with an Avery tractor. Like the Oil-Pull, the Aultman-Taylor and others, the Avery tractors used a heavyweight design comparable to the best engineering thought of the day. Yet, the new farm tractor industry was not only evolving, it was in a redhot flux! Change was constant, and designs were obsolescent almost before getting off the draftsman's table. Eventually, the interesting and attractive Avery tractor would fall victim to the same fate as the other heavyweights.

One of the first farm tractors to use a four-cylinder engine was the Big 4, built in 1904 by Gas Traction Company at Minneapolis. Except for the Hart-Parr, most other tractor builders of 1904 were using stationary gas engines adapted to a steam engine chassis. Thus, the Big 4 was indeed a radical departure from accepted practice. This model gained considerable popularity and also caught the eye of the powerful Emerson-Brantingham Company of Rockford, Illinois. The latter brought out the Big 4 line in 1912.

Huber Mfg. Company attempted to enter the farm tractor business in 1898. The company's first experiments were unsuccessful, and Huber made no further excursions until 1911, when a small "Farmer's Tractor" appeared. It had a short life and an unauspicious end, but prompted the company to move forward with improved designs. Huber continued in the tractor business until after World War II.

International Harvester Company was an early entrant into the farm tractor business. Their early designs were centered around the company's own stationary engines. IHC used the

LEFT:
Huber Manufacturing Company of Marion, Ohio, produced many tractors – including this early crank-started model – from 1911 until the 1940s.

ABOVE:
A 1906 International Harvester. Entering early into the farm tractor business, International Harvester spent significant time and money on research and design, and achieved great success as a consequence.

Morton Traction truck. This was a chassis that had been developed earlier by S. S. Morton and was intended for use with a stationary engine as a power plant. International Harvester achieved considerable success with this design and marketed several thousand of them, finally ending this design in 1917. Meanwhile, International Harvester was busily designing other tractors to suit farmers' needs. Relative to the industry, IHC probably spent as much as or more than any other tractor builder of the period in research and development work. This paid off in a big way for the company, since the returns far outweighed the expenditures.

During 1910 International Harvester launched two separate tractor lines: the Titan series and the Mogul line. Titan tractors were sold by Deering dealers and Mogul tractors were sold by McCormick implement dealers. After the 1902 merger that formed International Harvester, anti-trust suits had forced the company to operate as separate entities under the IHC corporate umbrella. This situation finally was resolved in 1919. In the interim, there were two separate tractor lines emerging from the International Harvester factories. Titan production was centered at the Milwaukee Works, and Mogul production was concentrated at the Chicago Works.

Significant also in the early development of the American farm tractor was the Twin City lines built by Minneapolis Steel & Machinery Company of Minneapolis, Minnesota. The company was organized in 1902 to build bridges and other steel products. During 1905 Minneapolis Steel also began building huge stationary gas engines. In 1910 the company built a few prototype copies of a large tractor. The amazing success of the prototypes led to full-scale production the following year. Twin City tractors continued apace until the company merged with another to form the Minneapolis-Moline Power Implement Company in 1929.

BELOW:
Two retired but significant players in the history of the American farm tractor: the Rumely OilPull and the Nichols & Shephard 25-50. The massive, kerosene-powered 25-50 was part of the Nichols & Shephard Red River Special line.

ABOVE:
With its enclosed engine and its operator's canopy, the Big Boss, a 20-35 built by Russell & Company, patrols the grounds at the Ozarks Steam Engine Festival.

Another of the old-line thresher builders to enter the tractor business was Nichols & Shepard Company at Battle Creek, Michigan. This company went back to 1848 as a thresher builder, and during the 1880s N & S began building steam traction engines. N & S resisted the emerging farmer preference for gas tractors over steam engines, but capitulated in 1911. The company's answer to the need for tractors was a massively built tractor rated at 35 drawbar and 70 belt horsepower. It used a two-cylinder engine with a 10½″ x 14″ bore and stroke. Rated speed was 375 rpm.

Farm tractor development up to 1910 centered around heavy, massive designs suited for plowing, threshing and similar applications. Almost all of them used the same stiff axle, chain-and-bolster steering so typical of the steam traction engine. Gearing was occasionally shielded, but most gears were fully exposed to dust, dirt and grit. Engines were mostly of the one- or two-cylinder style, operating at low speeds, and built of massive proportions. Almost none was equipped with a multiple speed gear drive; virtually every tractor built up to 1910 operated either forward or back, period. Some were capable of speeds up to 3 mph; the Aultman-Taylor had a top ground speed of 2 mph! Yet it was from these huge tractors that today's designs have evolved. In the 1910-1920 period the tractor industry would undergo a huge transformation; one that would relegate most of the heavyweight designs to obsolescence and replace them with small and lightweight models.

CHAPTER 2:
1910-1920

PAGES 24-25:
Farmers at work with a Samson tractor. The Samson was a product of General Motors' brief early interlude in the tractor-building business.

THE PERIOD UP TO 1910 saw dramatic developments in farm power. Huge tractors appeared, with the majority using various components developed originally for the steam traction engine. Companies like the Oliver Chilled Plow Works developed huge plows to match the tractors. The result was that huge American and Canadian prairies were converted to cropland. These enormous tractors were at the cutting edge of a new frontier in American history. Now that the prairies were being put under the plow, farmers were ready for smaller tractors. In addition to performing the perfunctory field work, farmers also wanted a tractor suitable for everyday farm tasks. The stage was being set for a new era of farm tractor development. Beginning about 1913 the small tractor came into its own. For a few years the demand was so strong that virtually any small tractor was saleable, even those of poor design.

In the period up to 1920, several hundred different tractor manufacturers appeared. In addition to the large, well established manufacturers, there were many more small firms. Some were successful, most were not. Unfortunately, a few of the small companies that built a very good tractor were unsuccessful in marketing their design. Many of the small companies were financially pressed to get a prototype tractor built, and simply did not have the resources or the expertise to advertise and promote their new design. Meanwhile, the large companies were capable of affording heavy promotion, full page advertisements, and persuasive salesmen. As the number of manufacturers increased, many companies withered from the heat of competition, while others flourished as never before.

Charlatans were also about. Several stock promotion schemes yielded large returns for the organizers, and after extracting considerable sums from trusting, and perhaps greedy, investors, they disappeared, along with the money entrusted to their care. A few of these companies actually built a prototype or two, and some simply failed due to bad management or a poor design.

A great many tractors of this period proved to be far less than was claimed by salesmen, promoters and magazine advertisements. Even worse, a farmer might buy one of these tractors one year, and when needing parts a few months later, discover that the company was no longer in business.

Nebraska legislator Wilmot F. Crozier has often been called the "Father of the Nebraska Tests." Crozier once wrote that "after operating or attempt-

RIGHT:
Port Huron Engine & Thresher Company of Port Huron, Michigan, had as its slogan, "Everything for the Thresherman." Established in 1851, by 1910 the company produced hay presses, plows, road makers, saw mills, wagons, threshers and traction engines such as this.

ing to operate two excuses for tractors, I finally invested my money in a machine that would really do what the company said it would. (At this point he bought a Rumely OilPull.) Then I began wondering if there wasn't some way to induce all tractor companies to tell the truth." The result was the Nebraska Tractor Test Law of 1919, which required all tractors sold in Nebraska to first undergo thorough and impartial testing by the Nebraska Tractor Test Laboratory. Tractor testing began at Lincoln in 1920. Over the years this facility has gained impeccable credentials and a worldwide reputation for its tractor testing activities.

As early as 1908, testing of tractors and steam traction engines had begun at the Winnipeg Industrial Exhibition. The test scores rated the entrants on their plowing, hauling and belt power capabilities. In 1909 the Winnipeg Trials included new categories for gas tractors. However, one editor in the farm press noted that the "test was a measure not only of the efficiency of the engine, but of the skill of the engineer in handling his machine as well." Subsequently, test procedures developed so that judgment calls and human errors were reduced insofar as possible.

By 1910 the Winnipeg Contests used a point system whereby each entry was rated on the basis of tangible evidence, such as horsepower hours derived from a unit of fuel. The Winnipeg Contests continued in 1913, but were losing their momentum. However, the Winnipeg Contests served the valuable purpose of teaching engineers how to properly and impartially test a tractor, and helping to enlighten farmers as to how they might choose a tractor to suit their needs. There was also an implicit message to manufacturers that farmers were looking for tractors capable of demonstrating quality.

ABOVE:
Responsive to the times, Avery Company of Peoria, Illinois, featured six tractor sizes in its 1918 Bulldog line, from the little 5-10 hp (pictured), suitable for small farms and reputed to replace the work of four horses, to the heavyweight 40-80 hp.

ABOVE:
Three International Harvesters plow side-by-side to demonstrate a new age in farm power. With several hundred tractor manufacturers appearing between 1910 and 1920, demonstrations of power farm equipment was a popular means for farmers to familiarize themselves with the various machines and their capabilities.

In September 1913 the first National Power Farming Demonstration was held at New Fremont, Nebraska. It was tremendously successful, and led to another demonstration at Fremont the following year. Huge crowds were in attendance, and tractor manufacturers were greatly buoyed by farmer enthusiasm. Over 60,000 people attended the 1915 demonstration in which 84 different tractors from 30 different companies were at work. The National Tractor & Thresher Manufacturers Association then made plans for a series of four-day demonstrations in 1916. The first one was held at Dallas, Texas, on July 7, 1916. In sequence, the same act was replayed at Hutchinson, Kansas; St. Louis, Missouri; Cedar Rapids, Iowa; Bloomingdale, Illinois; Madison, Wisconsin; Fargo, North Dakota; and Aberdeen, South Dakota. After this the enthusiasm in tractor demonstrations waned, and farmers were again left to defend themselves as best they could against poor designs and unscrupulous manufacturers.

The concept of a National Testing Station appeared by 1915, or even earlier. The U.S. Congress was slow to move on this subject, and after bureaucratic wrangling, never made any headway. Meanwhile, Ohio State University conducted a series of tests in 1919. At this point, the Nebraska Tractor Test Law came into effect. From then on, farmers everywhere looked to the Nebraska Tractor Tests as a reliable yardstick of tractor performance.

The decade of 1910-1920 was indeed one of dramatic change. Farmers were getting their first taste of power farming, and liking it. Not only could a farmer produce more grain with a much lower expenditure of time, he could also do it with much less hand labor than ever before in history. There was now no doubt that the small tractor was here to stay!

Another area of change and refinement was that of design. During the decade of 1910-1920, virtually every idea emerged for tractor design. Every possible wheel configuration was used, and tractors were equipped with an unending variety of engines. Although most of the designs faded within a decade, in favor of a conventional four-wheel arrangement, these many different ideas convincingly proved what would work and what wouldn't work.

Beginning the new era of small farm

tractors was the Bull, built by Bull Tractor Company in Minneapolis. Announced in September 1913, the Bull retailed at only $335, or about one-tenth the price of a 30-60 Rumely OilPull. Rated at 5 drawbar and 12 belt horsepower, the Bull could pull a single plow and other small farm equipment. It was also suitable for light belt work around the farm.

Despite its rather poor and unconventional design, the Bull was an immediate sensation. In seven months' time the company sold 3,800 of these little tractors. All of the company organizers were veterans of the tractor business. They all knew that the industry had been selling too much iron for too little money, and that quite often, they weren't getting the money. The Bull was designed with less iron and sold for less money, but the cardinal rule was to get the money. These tractors were sold on a cash basis only; there was no extended payment plan as had always been the rule in the tractor business.

Actually, the concept of cash selling came from the developing automobile business. On the other hand, the farm implement business had long been characterized by a small down payment and extended terms. This plan developed decades earlier when reaper and thresher builders offered extended payment plans as an inducement to sell their machines. It would take many decades to bring the farm equipment business into a cash basis.

Perhaps more than any other, the Bull tractor changed the face of American farm tractor design. The big tractors of the past were doomed to obsolescence, and the concept of a small and efficient farm tractor was now a reality.

Like its larger ancestors, the Bull tractor used a steel frame. All components of engine and drive train were mounted separately on the frame. Reason dictated that the tractor would be far more efficient and would weigh much less if the engine and drive train were built as a single unit. Thus came the unit frame design, now accepted as standard practice.

In 1913 the Wallis Cub tractor appeared. This model used a frame made of rolled boilerplate. The rear part of the frame carried the transmission and final drives, while the front portion served as the engine crankcase. All gearing was maintained in perfect alignment due to the rigidity of the frame. All gears operated in an oil bath, securely protected from dirt and other contaminants. While unauspicious in itself, the Wallis Cub made tractor history by being the first tractor built with a unit frame. In 1915 the Wallis Cub Junior appeared, and this

TOP:
Tractor innovations of the decade were as numerous as were tractor manufacturers. This farmer plows straight lines with the help of a guide wheel in 1916.

ABOVE:
The 1920 Rumely OilPull 16-30 was a horsepower upgrade of the 14-28 introduced in 1918.

and an agreement was made whereby the Ford name could be used in connection with the tractor. Thus, when Henry Ford developed his tractor in 1917, he was prevented from selling it as a Ford, since this name was already in use as a registered trademark of the Ford Tractor Company. Henry's new tractor then became the Fordson. The Fordson went on to great fame, while the Ford went on to infamy. Few Ford Tractors were built, despite the many thousands of dollars paid in by investors. One of those persons associated with Ford Tractor Company was later sentenced for conspiracy to defraud investors, and another was reported to have organized a tractor company in Canada following the bankruptcy of the Ford operation.

TOP:
The Wallis Cub made history by being the first tractor with a unit frame.

ABOVE:
Henry Ford first experimented with tractors in 1907, then mass-produced the light, gas-powered Fordson in 1917.

OPPOSITE TOP:
The 10-28 Case of 1919.

OPPOSITE BOTTOM:
International Harvester's 15-30 was part of the company's 1918 offerings.

model even had the final drives enclosed and running in oil! Wallis tractors were built by the J. I. Case Plow Works at Racine, Wisconsin. This company had no corporate connection to the J. I. Case Threshing Machine Company, also of Racine, that manufactured the Case tractor line. Wallis tractors continued using their patented boilerplate frame until they sold out to Massey-Harris in 1928. Subsequently, Massey-Harris continued with the boilerplate frame design into the early 1940s.

The Ford Tractor Company was organized at Minneapolis about 1915. The idea ostensibly was to capitalize on Henry Ford's name and reputation, so a man by the name of Ford was located,

Henry Ford made automotive history with the Model T Ford automobile. More than any other car, the Model T put an increasingly mobile America on wheels. Ford's dream of a cheap and reliable automobile was exactly what Americans were looking for, and Model T's were part and parcel of American life. Ford now concentrated his efforts on building a small tractor suitable for virtually every American farm.

Already in 1907 Ford had built an experimental model of a small lightweight tractor, but it was never marketed. However, in 1916 his first experimental model appeared of a new cast iron unit frame design. Ford was quick to claim that his new tractor was the first to utilize the unit frame, but in fact, he had been pre-empted by the Wallis Cub. The only major difference was in the materials used. Ford used a cast iron unit frame, while the Wallis Club used one fabricated from steel boilerplate.

By 1918 the Fordson tractor was in full production. Despite its design flaws, it was immensely popular from its inception. In fact, of the 133,000 farm tractors built in 1918, Ford led the field with a production of over 34,000 units. The previously untouchable International Harvester Company came in second, with the rest of the in-

dustry trailing behind. No longer was it possible to conduct business as usual in the tractor business. Particularly due to the strong showing of the Fordson, the entire industry was thrown into a decade of intensive and oftentimes cutthroat competition. When the smoke cleared from what might be described as The Great Tractor War, the field was littered with casualties. Ultimately, it was the farmer who won the victory. Intense competition had yielded new and extremely useful tractor designs.

Fordson tractors had their own special idiosyncracies. For instance, they used the same vibrator coils for ignition as were found on the Model T automobile. Failure to maintain the coil points often led to problems. The worm gear final drive was capable of generating intense heat on drawbar work. This kept the operator's feet uncomfortably warm, and the pressed steel seat directly over the final drive served to warm the operator's backside as well. The Fordson had a propensity to overheat, and some farmers were openly incredulous that an engine could get to hot in the summer and still freeze up in the winter. A governor came as an extra cost option, and a belt pulley came only as extra equipment. There were no fenders, and the operator inhaled most of the dirt coming from the drivewheels.

These and other problems prompted the United States Department of Agriculture to send their Professor Arnold Yerkes to Michigan on an evaluation study of the Fordson. Yerkes spend considerable time drafting a report. When submitted to his superiors, the report was quite unfavorable to the Fordson. The USDA decided to suppress the report. As so often happens with secrets, this one leaked out, and the farm press provided its subscribers with some interesting and controversial reading for several months.

A nationwide depression occurred in the early 1920s. This, combined with a saturation of the tractor market, brought competition to new heights. Ford dropped the price of the Fordson to $395 in February 1922. International Harvester countered by dropping the price of the 10-20 Titan tractor to $700 and throwing in a plow or a disk for free. Finally, even the bank accounts of Henry Ford could not sustain the continued sales of a tractor at something less than its production cost. In 1928, domestic production of

BELOW:
International Harvester's Titan 10-20 demonstrates its versatility. Belt power could be used for such work as silage cutting, threshing, feed grinding, bailing, pumping and sawing.

the Fordson tractor ended, and with it, a most colorful era in the chronology of American farm tractor development.

The Allis-Chalmers Company was another major player in the farm tractor industry. Tremendously diverse, Allis-Chalmers had previously achieved worldwide recognition in the power industry. Steam engines, steam turbines, hydraulic turbines and electrical generators were but a part of the Allis-Chalmers operation. Yet, Colonel Falk at the helm of Allis-Chalmers was determined to put a tractor on the market. In 1914 the 10-18 tractor appeared. Although it was never a booming sales success, it launched the company into the tractor business, even in the face of withering competition.

Subsequent to the 10-18 came the 18-30 model; during its 10-year production run, ending in 1929, there were some 16,000 units built. Allis-Chalmers would later broaden its position in the tractor industry through the acquisition of the Advance-Rumely Thresher Company at LaPorte, Indiana. Advance-Rumely had, in turn, bought out Aultman & Taylor Machinery Company in 1924.

LEFT:
An Allis-Chalmers 6-12 from 1919. Allis-Chalmers entered the tractor business in 1914, with its 10-18. The smaller 6-12 was produced from 1919 to 1923.

LEFT:
This canopied Aultman-Taylor was one of the company's versatile tractors that combined strength and durability. Located in Mansfield, Ohio, Aultman-Taylor was taken over by Advance-Rumely in 1924.

ABOVE:
A Rumely OilPull demonstrates its belt power.

BELOW:
Avery's 40-80 was the company's largest tractor in 1914.

Advance-Rumely had become a major player in the farm tractor business with their Rumely OilPull. This unique and thoroughly reliable tractor first emerged in 1910. Expansionism had resulted in the acquisition of numerous companies by 1912. However, crop failures, bad paper and a changing tractor industry forced this gigantic company into receivership during 1915. It soon reorganized as the Advance-Rumely Thresher Company, but the reorganized firm never achieved the financial returns or the glory of earlier years. One of the company's greatest moments came in 1911. At Purdue University, three Rumely OilPulls were hitched to a 50 bottom Oliver plow, turning over some three rods of earth at a single pass. Farmers of the time were mightily impressed with this feat, especially since the vast majority had never seen anything larger than a two-bottom gang plow, pulled by five horses.

Tractor directories published in the period up to 1920 yield dozens and dozens of firms ostensibly intended to provide a good tractor to the farmer and a nice checkbook balance for the organizers. One such tractor was the Andrews, built at Minneapolis. Priced at $575, it was of the three-wheel design and capable of 20 brake horse-

LEFT:
John Deere purchased the Waterloo Gas Engine Company in 1918 and continued to produce the Waterloo Boy. This Waterloo Boy Model N from 1919 sports John Deere colors, and its well built design was essentially unchanged from its earlier days.

power. Meanwhile, the Avery Company at Peoria, Illinois, was making its own noise with an exceptionally large line of tractors.

Avery Company went back to the 1870s, and began building steam traction engines in 1893. The Avery Yellow Fellow threshing machines were well known throughout the United States and Canada. Avery got into the tractor business in 1911. By 1914 the line ranged from a small 8-16 model up to the huge 40-80. Avery even countered the Fordson threat with their little 5-10 tractor, first offered in 1916. This one initially sold for $295, even less than the price of the Fordson tractor. Avery also trailblazed their way into a new tractor design, the motor cultivator. In 1916 the first Avery motor cultivator appeared. This machine was built around the little 5-10 tractor, and was primarily intended for cultivating row crops. Here was the first successful attempt to cultivate with tractor power, marking the beginning of a new era in the farm power business. However, the Avery and other motor cultivators of the time were only partially successful. Farmers wanted a tractor that could combine all the elements needed for year-round farming into a single and very adaptable tractor. Achieving these goals would take a few more years.

J. I. Case Threshing Machine Company joined the ranks of the tractor builders in 1911. By 1913 the company was building three different models of a conventional four-wheel design. However, in 1915 the company introduced their 10-20 model, a three-wheeled design, ostensibly intended to counter the tremendous popularity of the Bull and several other tractors of the latter style. This one remained on the market for a few years, but the company's first move toward a lightweight design came with the 1916 introduction of their 9-18 model.

Case went a step further with the 10-18 tractor, first sold in 1918. It adopted the unit frame design, and resulted in a very compact tractor. The 10-18 and its contemporaries all used a crossmounted engine, and this feature permitted a very simple design for the drive train. The largest of the Case crossmounts was the 40-72, capable of nearly 50 drawbar horsepower.

Many companies remained in the market with well built tractor designs, changing them but little in the 1910-1920 period. Included in this category was the Waterloo Boy, first built by the Waterloo Gasoline Engine Company. Deere & Company in Moline, Illinois, bought out this firm in 1918, and continued to market the Waterloo Boy, essentially unchanged from its former features and appearance. Likewise, the Hart-Parr Company at Charles City, Iowa, introduced its New Hart-Parr in 1918, and this led to an entire series of tractors with an uncanny resemblance to the Waterloo Boy.

RIGHT: Available by mail-order, Galloway's Bear-Cat 10-20 tractor sold for $1,495.

Questions still are raised among vintage tractor enthusiasts regarding the design similarities of these two tractor models.

Although the 1910-1920 period in American farm tractor development was crowned with a few success stories, it was also colored by many more disastrous tales. Thousands of speculators invested millions of dollars with the goal of achieving their own brand of success. Most of them failed, with financial disaster and personal pain being their compensation. Typical of these stories is that of the Denning tractor.

Denning Motor Implement Company was organized at Cedar Rapids, Iowa, in 1913. It resulted from experiments conducted by Joseph Denning as early as 1908. From the outset, Denning sought to build a small, lightweight tractor suitable for the average farm. In fact, many of his advertisements billed it as "The Denning Light Farm Tractor."

Denning had amassed a sizeable fortune with his patents on fence-weaving machinery. This allowed him to expend a substantial amount of money on tractor development, and several styles appeared in the period up to 1916. That year he came out with the Model E. It featured a hood over the engine, and it used an enclosed transmission case. The spring-mounted front axle was an innovative feature borrowed from automotive design, and in fact, much of the Model E tractor was built around automotive developments.

Within its class, the Denning was probably as good as most of the tractors on the 1916 market, and undoubtedly better than some of the competition. But the Denning sold poorly, and simply could not compete with tractors like the $395 Bull or the $295 Avery 5-10. Even by cutting costs to the bone, the 10-18 sold at $800, or more than twice the cost of some of its peers. Against these and other problems, the Model E took Denning into bankruptcy. After another brief business venture, Joseph Denning spent his final years in obscurity.

A similar situation occurred with the Galloway tractor built at Waterloo, Iowa. The William Galloway tractor achieved national renown with its mail-order business. Galloway specialized in stationary gasoline engines, and the Galloway catalog carried hundreds of implements and farm items.

Galloway's "Farmobile" tractor first appeared in 1916. Due in part to this tractor, Galloway went bankrupt in 1920. When the company was reorganized, William Galloway was no longer a member of the firm.

Also of interest in the remarkable decade of 1910-20 was the entry of General Motors Corporation into the tractor market. William C. Durant, the chairman of General Motors, was determined to meet the Fordson challenge. If it wasn't enough that Ford had nearly cornered the automobile market with his Model T, he was now threatening to take over the tractor market with the Fordson. Thus, General Motors bought a plant at Janesville , Wisconsin, to build their Samson tractor. The original designs came from the Samson Tractor Works of Stockton, California. General Motors bought out this company in 1917. GMC experienced huge losses in its tractor venue, got out of the tractor business in 1922, and converted the Janesville plant to a Chevrolet assembly operation.

International Harvester Company made tractor history in the 1910-1920 period with its Mogul and Titan tractor lines. Both operated under the IHC corporate umbrella, but the two product lines were distinctly different. IHC also pioneered their motor cultivator in 1916, and although it could hardly be classified as a success, the IHC motor cultivator would eventually become the progenitor of the Farmall row crop tractor.

There are many other interesting companies that emerged in the 1910-1920 period. One of particular note was the Moline Plow Company. This firm went all the way back to 1852, and had built a solid business over the years. In 1915 Moline bought out the

BELOW:
International Harvester's 22 hp Titan from 1919 was but one of the company's many offerings. The Titan and Mogul product lines both operated under International Harvester's corporate umbrella.

LEFT:
International Harvester's innovative motor cultivator of 1916 was built and sold for only a short time, but would eventually become the progenitor of the Farmall row-crop tractor.

ABOVE:
Discing his cornfield in 1918, a farmer adapts his Avery tractor with a pelt for a seat cushion and rocks to weigh down the discer.

RIGHT:
International Harvester's successful 1914 Mogul 8-16 provided a versatile power source for America's farms.

LEFT:
An early crawler, the Cleveland "20" of 1916 was one of the company's first tractors. From 1918 on Cleveland's tractors were renamed "Cletracs."

Universal Cultivator Company. From their design came the Moline Universal tractor. This unique machine placed the drivewheels to the front, with the engine situated between them. An entire line of implements evolved, all designed for use with the tractor. Many were adapted directly from horsedrawn implements.

The Moline Universal was equipped with electric starting, electric lights and an electric governor. Even though it was capable of over 27 belt horsepower, the Moline Universal weighed but 3,380 pounds, and this was a major advancement in reducing the total weight of farm tractors. Despite its erstwhile popularity, the Moline Universal disappeared from the scene by 1923.

In retrospect, the 1910-1920 period saw the transformation from huge, unwieldy tractors to much smaller and much lighter designs. This transformation would continue, and in fact, continues on to the present time. The reduction of engine weight, or properly the weight to horsepower ratio, gained significant ground in this decade. While some of the heavyweights had an operating speed of under 400 rpm, the Moline Universal, for example, had a top-rated speed of 1,800 rpm. Raising the compression also gained additional power. Steel cut and shaved gears reduced friction, as did the use of ball and roller bearings. The unit frame was beginning to replace the iron frame with separate mountings of engine and drive train. Four-cylinder engines were gaining in popularity over the one- and two-cylinder styles. The 1910-1920 decade was indeed a delightful period of farm tractor development. The next 10 years would see the loss of many tractor manufacturers, but would also herald the beginning of many new and innovative ideas, including that of the Farmall row-crop tractor.

BELOW:
The innovative Moline Universal tractor, produced from 1915 until 1923, featured electric starting, electric lights, and 27-belt horsepower.

CHAPTER 3:
The 1920s

PAGES 40-41:
Indiana farmers cut and bind wheat with the John Deere Model D tractor and power binder.

BELOW:
The Cleveland Tractor Company promotes the profit potential of its Cletrac crawler on its catalog cover.

BY THE TIME 1920 arrived, tractor building was at its zenith, at least in terms of the number of companies on board. However, several factors were already at work which spelled doom for the vast majority of them over the next decade. The first was the post-war financial depression of the early 1920s. For a while at least, farmers hesitated to buy anything more than necessary. Many companies were operating on a shoestring, and simply didn't have the resources to wait for good times to return. The market was becoming saturated, so sales were slowing down. Farmers were also becoming very discriminating about the tractors they bought; there were too many horror stories floating around about how someone got taken with a tractor that proved to be something less than advertised.

Enter the Nebraska Tractor Test Law in 1919. Although the new law affected only tractors sold within Nebraska, the test procedures were based on the best available scientific procedures. The farm press took note of the tests, and tractor builders over the years have often cited tests on a particular tractor model, especially when it was advantageous to their own cause. However, partial citations from the test reports were not permitted; if a manufacturer wished to cite the report, law required that the entire report be printed. The great benefit was that now there was a means whereby farm tractors could be fairly and impartially tested. The test results were public information, and farmers soon picked up on which tractors made a good performance, and which ones did badly. The *Tractor Red Book* and the *Farm Implement News Buyer's Guide* both published the test reports each year, so they assumed national importance almost immediately. There is no doubt that the Nebraska Tractor Tests profoundly affected the farm tractor industry and provided immense benefits to the farmers who were in need of tractor power.

A sidebar benefit of the Nebraska Tractor Tests is that they have provided a valuable historical record. The original Nebraska Tractor Test files contained information seldom found elsewhere. To the credit of the Nebraska Tractor Test Laboratory, each and every tractor test report remains intact.

The majority of the tractors built in the 1920-1930 period used kerosene fuel. It was cheap compared to gasoline, so it was ideal from the cost standpoint. However, kerosene had numerous disadvantages. It was virtually impossible to start an engine directly on kerosene. Instead, gasoline was used for starting, and after the engine warmed up a bit, it was switched over to kerosene. When running under any kind of load, it was imperative that water be added to the air/fuel mixture to retard preignition. Failure to do so resulted in poor running, blown head gaskets, and unsatisfactory performance. In freezing climates, many farmers switched over to high-test gasoline during the winter months. Various methods were used to break up the kerosene into a vapor, but its chemical makeup is such that it atomizes, but does not vaporize like gasoline. Thus came all kinds and styles of preheating devices. Some worked and some didn't. Regardless of the methods used, problems persisted with crankcase dilution, due to the unburned kerosene fuel in the engine cylinders. A study of the Nebraska Tractor Tests indicates that virtually everything submitted prior to the late 1920s was built for use with kerosene fuel. By this time, new high speed and high compression engines were coming into their own, and many of these could be equipped to burn kerosene or gasoline as a buyer's option. By the mid-1930s kerosene was falling into disuse in favor of gasoline. A small revival occurred at that time for distillate, the latter being slightly better than kerosene, but not nearly so good as gasoline. It was somewhat popular for a few years, but was eventually abandoned.

Tractors of the unit frame design were becoming more evident. The majority of new tractors coming onto the 1920s market followed this pattern. The four-cylinder engine was becoming more popular, but the Avery Model C used a six-cylinder engine. This model was tested at Nebraska in 1920 under Test No. 39, and was the first six-cylinder tractor ever tested at Lincoln. It also featured a three-speed transmission at a time when many tractors had only two forward speeds plus reverse.

Crawler tractors – equipped with continuous roller belts over cogged wheels – were gaining in popularity, especially the Cletrac models from Cleveland Tractor Company. Cletrac was the first major builder to tailor a series of implements, including front-mounted cultivators, to its crawlers. The Cletrac Model W, 12-20, was the first crawler tested at Nebraska; it appears under Test No. 45 of July 1920. Numerous other small crawlers were available, including the Bates Steel Mule, and the Avery Track Runner. In addition, there were several companies building crawler attachments whereby a standard wheel tractor could be converted to a crawler. Typical of these was the Trackpull. It was built by the Belle City Manufacturing Company at Racine, Wisconsin, and was especially designed for use with the Fordson tractor. In addition to these, several different models

TOP:
Continuous roller belts are noticeably absent on this early experimental crawler tractor, built on a 9-16 chassis.

ABOVE:
With rear fenders and an enclosed hood, Appleton's 12-20 tractor's body design resembled that of an automobile.

TOP:
The Cletrac Model F featured a compact design. Suitable for small farms, the Model F was built from 1920 to 1922.

ABOVE:
The Bates Steel Mule Model G crawler tractor featured independent front drive wheels.

appeared of the Monarch crawlers. These were built by Monarch Tractors, a firm that was later taken over by Allis-Chalmers, forming the basis of the extensive A-C crawler line.

In 1925 the Caterpillar Tractor Company was formed from a merger of the Holt and Best interests. Although Caterpillar and its predecessors were also building small crawlers for farm use, their major emphasis was on large tractors designed for heavy construction. Holt submitted their 40-60 tractor to Nebraska in 1920, where it delivered over 57 brake horsepower. A few months later the Best 60 was tested, and it yielded 55 brake horsepower. Of their small crawlers built in the 1920s, the Caterpillar Two-Ton was one of the most popular for farm work. It was capable of about 15 drawbar horsepower, and used gasoline fuel. The terms "Cat" and "Caterpillar" are registered trademarks of Caterpillar Tractor Company.

During 1922 and 1923 International Harvester Company launched their 15-30 and 10-20 tractors in that order. Almost overnight, these two tractors became extremely popular. They featured the company's own four-cylinder valve-in-head engine, and as an industry first, these models used ball bearings for the mains. The crankshaft was designed without a center main, thus permitting the relatively easy use of the ball bearings at each end. The company was so confident of this design that the ball bearings were guaranteed for the life of the tractor. Rare indeed was the case in which they had to be replaced.

In September 1925 the McCormick-Deering Farmall tractor was tested at Nebraska under No. 117. This was the first true row-crop tractor to be tested. The development of the Farmall is a story in itself. Just when International Harvester began experimenting with an all-purpose row-crop tractor is not known. The Company built a motor-driven harvesting machine as early as 1902, and in 1910 outlined a lightweight machine that could push or pull a binder, corn husker or various other machines. Sometime prior to 1915 the company built the first of several experimental tractors that eventually led to the IHC Motor Cultivator of 1916. Between that time and 1922, IHC built the motor cultivator in several versions. In addition, it was used within the company's experimental program with an eye toward development of an all-purpose tractor. During 1918 the company mounted a grain binder to the motor cultivator chassis. In so doing, a power take-off drive was devised, and this was one of the first attempts within the industry to utilize power in such a manner. McCormick-Deering 15-30 tractors of 1921 featured an optional pto shaft. From these simple beginnings came today's commonly accepted pto drives. However, it is important to note that the pto output shaft actually had its beginnings with the motor cultivator experiments of 1918, and perhaps even earlier.

The term "Farmall" was first used by

BELOW LEFT:
The Trackpull crawler attachment converted this 27 hp Fordson into a crawler tractor.

BELOW:
After the race to develop an all-purpose tractor in the 1920s, International Harvester came out with its big McCormick-Deering WK-40 in 1934.

OPPOSITE TOP:
John Deere's two-cylinder GP (General Purpose) model, which began production in the late 1920s, was rated at 20 horsepower.

OPPOSITE BOTTOM:
A bucolic scene from John Deere's calendar features the GP model.

ABOVE RIGHT:
The front grille of John Deere's Model D became a familiar face on America's farms. Introduced in 1923 and manufactured for decades, the Model D would achieve the longest production run in tractor history.

BELOW:
John Deere's two-cylinder Model D packed a lot of power into its compact design.

International Harvester in 1919. The experimental models of that time had almost no resemblance to the Farmall tractor that would later emerge. However, the term itself is indicative of the company's intentions to develop and market an all-purpose row-crop tractor. In fact, company records indicate that the term "Motor Cultivator" was last used about 1920. Another 1919 improvement was the addition of a power lift system. It too would become a salient feature of many tractors in the 1930s.

In perspective, the development of the all-purpose tractor required a complete rethinking of farm implement design. Up to this time, almost all implements were designed for use with horses or mules. Mowers and other machines were operated through a ground drive. The idea of tractor power forced designers back to the drafting table. In some cases, implements could be modified slightly for effective use with the tractor. In other situations, they required a complete redesign. The problem was that the all-purpose tractor and its implements had to be designed simultaneously,

and ultimately, the tractor had to be capable of handling all the mounted or towed implements with relative ease.

Sometime in 1920 the motor cultivator was again revised so that the resulting prototype began to take on a vague resemblance to what eventually would become the Farmall tractor. At this point it still seemed desirable to build a reversible tractor, that is, one which could be operated with the drive wheels forward or behind, as circumstances required. This idea was abandoned by 1921. The 1922 experimental models were now taking on the general appearance of the Farmall, and in 1923 the company authorized 22 of these tractors to be built as prototypes. The company also put the official title of "Farmall" on the new tractor design. In 1924 International Harvester executives authorized 200 Farmall tractors, and over 100 of these were sold by July 1 of that year. Although these tractors sold for $825, a substantial price in those days, they actually were sold at a considerable loss, since each of them was essentially built by hand. A Farmall production line was not in place until the following year, and even with the reductions in manufacturing costs, the 1924 price for the Farmall was $950.

From its beginnings, the Farmall was available with numerous implements and attachments built especially for use with the tractor. Contrary to the accepted industry norm, the Farmall was not horsepower rated, although in Nebraska Tractor Test No. 117 it delivered 12 drawbar and 18 belt horsepower. The company used its own four-cylinder valve-in-head engine with a bore and stroke of 3¾" x 5". Rated speed was 1,200 rpm. The little Farmall weighed just over 4,000 pounds.

Deere & Company made tractor history with their 1923 introduction of the venerable Model D. It would remain in production for decades, and achieved the longest production run of any tractor ever built. This unique two-cylinder design utilized unit frame construction and gave a small and compact design. Even though it weighed only 4,200 pounds, the Model D was capable of about 30 belt horsepower. However, the Model D was a standard-tread style, and this limited its use for row-crop work. In other words, it was no competition for the Farmall. Then, in 1928, Deere countered with the GP (General Purpose) model rated at 10 drawbar and 20 belt horsepower. It was of standard-tread design, but used an arched front axle for clearance above growing corps. Deere complemented this design with a series of three-row implements that even included a planter and cultivator.

J. I. Case Company closed out its famous crossmotor tractors with the 1929 introduction of their Model C and Model L designs. Using four-cylinder engines manufactured in the Case factories, these unit frame tractors gained an early reputation for power and reliability. Also in 1929, Case introduced their Model CC tractor, the company's first row-crop design. With it the company offered an extensive variety of specially designed implements. In following the chronology of American farm tractor development, the argument can rightfully be presented that this was the first real competition to the Farmall of International Harvester Company. Soon there would be more!

The decade of the 1920s was one of

ABOVE:
A farmer plows his cornfield with his Case Model CC. Introduced in 1929, the Model CC was Case's first row-crop tractor.

BELOW:
Emerson-Brantingham advertised its 12-20 Model AA kerosene tractor in 1923 as "a small tractor with big power . . . especially designed for operation by women or boys."

profound change, much like those before it. Yet, the changes that occurred were very progressive, and all were a part of an evolutionary process. Up to 1920 the majority of Americans lived on farms or in rural areas. In the 1920s the population came to be about equally divided, and this was evidence that the face of American agriculture, and indeed, America itself, was changing from an agrarian to an urban society. Due to power farming, one man could do the work that formerly required several. Horses and mules were assuming less importance as the power source on the farm. After all, it was easier to crank the tractor and perform a small task than it was to get the team into the barn, harness them, and get hooked up to a wagon.

The farm press and agricultural colleges contributed mightily to the changing face of American agriculture. Tractor power was encouraged, but that was only a part of the picture. Farmers were also shown the positive benefits of improved farming practices such as crop rotation and the proper use of lime and commercial fertilizers. Agronomists were busy developing improved varieties of corn and other grains. Plants could be bred to accentuate their resistance to various diseases and pests. The improved seed varieties led to bigger yields, as did the new farming practices that were emerging. These new trends, coupled with the advent of tractor power, permitted a farmer to be more efficient and productive than at any time in history.

Although most farmers thought that steam power would certainly have specialized uses on the farm, very few ever thought that it would disappear entirely. Few farmers of the 1920s

could visualize that horse power of the animate kind would almost completely disappear from American farm life. The coming of the automobile, especially those millions of Model T Ford cars, necessitated the building of roads. Local farmers often banded together to grade the roads in their area, each taking their turn at leveling out the ruts left after the last rain. At last, rural America was becoming mobile, and this provided better transportation for farm produce, whether it was the fatted calves or surplus grain. In other words, the farm tractor was a part of a much larger scene. Without the essential element of farm power and the farm tractor, America's transformation from an agrarian to an urban economy would have taken much longer. The decade of the 1920s was certainly one of change, and those who were involved probably never understood the transformation taking place before their very eyes.

Tractor development itself was undergoing tremendous change, exemplified in the emergence of the Farmall all-purpose row-crop tractor. By 1930 a few other companies were thinking along the same lines, and even fewer had countered the competition presented by the Farmall. Unit frame design was becoming the rule rather than the exception, and the power take-off drive was becoming a reality. Power lift systems were in their infancy and would become common within a decade. A few manufacturers had even gone so far as to streamline their tractors with louvered hoods to protect the engine and enhance the appearance. All of these, and many other factors, set the stage for even greater and more dynamic changes in the 1930s.

TOP:
In 1921 the Russell & Company of Massillon, Ohio, produced its gas tractor in four sizes, ranging from 12-24 to 30-60.

ABOVE:
In 1926 Hart-Parr produced the small and versatile 12-24 Model E.

LEFT:
One of America's most successful tractors, the popular Fordson Model F sold about 100,000 units a year in the early 1920s.

CHAPTER 4:
The 1930s

PAGES 50-51:
A farmer harvests corn with help from Allis-Chalmers.

THE 1930S SAW ENTIRELY new farm tractor designs. From over 200 different manufacturers in 1920, the field had shrunk to a few dozen, and some of these were hanging on by their thumbnails. As if from a gigantic smelter's furnace, the tractor industry had been refined and reduced from a multitude of impractical designs to a highly efficient power source.

Significant moves toward standardization did not come until the 1930. Prior to that time, there were no industry standards for drawbar height, pto shaft sizes, or belt pulley designs. Much of the pioneering work in standardization resulted from the efforts of the American Society of Agricultural Engineers. In addition, the Nebraska Tractor Tests did much to point out the advantages and disadvantages of various designs.

During the 1920s steam power was coming to an end. Many of the earlier steam traction engine builders dropped out of sight, and other moved into the tractor business. A. D. Baker Company at Swanton, Ohio, introduced their 16-30 steam tractor in 1921, but very few were built. Farmers were not inclined toward the extra time and effort required by steam power.

Faulty ignition was one of the major problems with early tractors. A weak magneto made the engine hard to start, and this was a constant frustration to the farmer. Companies sprang up that specialized in magneto building, with names like Bosch, K-W,

BELOW:
The Case Model L demonstrates the usefulness of its belt power, moving hay into a barn loft in 1933.

Dixie, Eisemann, Splitdorf, and Simms becoming commonly known. Fairbanks-Morse Company entered the magneto business in the 1920s, ostensibly to use on their own stationary engines. However, the F-M designs were of such high quality that this firm began building magnetos for virtually all applications during the 1930s. Fairbanks-Morse had used a series of different magnetos on their engines in years past, but always with considerable service problems. Likewise, J. I. Case Company began building their own magnetos during the 1930s, as did International Harvester Company. Spark plugs were also improved during the 1930s.

Lubrication, or the lack thereof, was a constant problem. Cylinder lubrication was initially effected by the use of a gravity feed lubricator which was regulated by hand. By 1910 the force-feed lubricator came into use, and many tractor engines used this method into the 1920s, while a very few persisted into the early 1930s. Hart-Parr Company promoted the concept of once-through lubrication. A force-feed lubricator took care of the pistons and mains. Surplus oil drained off from the engine crankcase and traveled to the final drive gear. Eventually the oil made its way back to the earth from whence it came. Although this method sounds waste-

ABOVE:
John Deere's GP was one of the decade's many row-crop tractors.

LEFT:
International Harvester's Farmall F20 engine burned either distillate or kerosene.

LEFT:
McCormick-Deering's Farmall Regular was IH's original row-crop model, and sold steadily from its inception in 1924 through the early 1930s.

ful by today's standards, it should be remembered that few tractors of 1930 were equipped with oil filters.

Borrowing from the automotive industry, tractor builders began adapting lubricating systems to their own designs. Much of this work was developed by the Society of Automotive Engineers and the American Society of Mechanical Engineers. From these early efforts came full pressure lubrication with drilled crankshafts, and pressure lubrication of cam bearings and mains. Meanwhile, lubricants were improved. The early years saw substantial quantities of poor quality lubricants, many of which were sold to an unsuspecting public by smooth-talking salesmen.

Poor lubrication and dust were then, and are now, the great enemies of the tractor engine. Few tractors prior to 1930 had an air cleaner. During the 1920s the "air washer" gained a certain amount of popularity. It pulled intake air through a water bath on its way to the engine cylinders. The air washer trapped large quantities of dirt and other debris but was relatively inefficient. Finally, in the 1930s the oil bath air cleaner was developed. It was the best answer that the industry had yet seen to providing a clean air supply to the tractor engine.

Cooling systems underwent considerable development during the 1920s. At the time, most tractor radiators boiled away large quantities of water, and most cooling systems were of the natural or thermosyphon type. Improved radiator designs, efficient fans, and the addition of water-circulating pumps all aided in providing the cooling needed for efficient engine operation. Thermostats came into use during the 1930s to provide accurate temperature regulation.

Prior to 1930, a number of transmission types were used. For a time, the friction drive transmission gained some popularity. Its chief advantage was that it provided infinitely variable speeds, and this concept was not to attain fruition for another 30 years. Up to the 1920s, the majority of tractors moved only forward and backward, but eventually the multiple speed transmission came into use. At first there were two or three forward speeds available, but by 1930, several tractors were being built with four forward speeds. In another decade the majority of tractors offered four forward speeds as a minimum.

Tractor designers had long thought of rubber tires and in fact, International Harvester Company had attempted this design in 1918. The effort failed, but provided the impetus

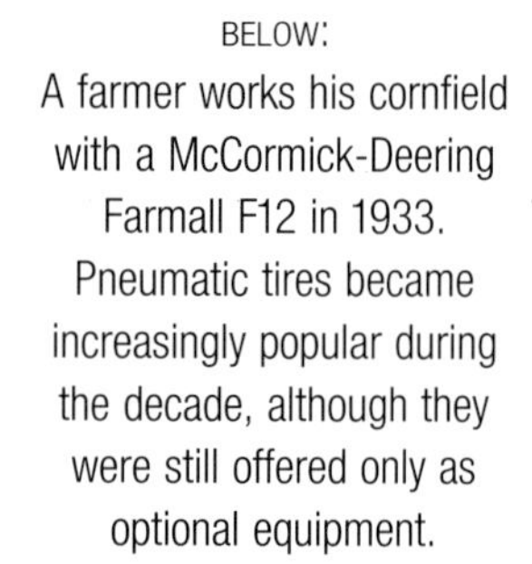

BELOW:
A farmer works his cornfield with a McCormick-Deering Farmall F12 in 1933. Pneumatic tires became increasingly popular during the decade, although they were still offered only as optional equipment.

ABOVE:
In 1932 Allis-Chalmers was the first company to offer pneumatic tires on its tractors. This lanky and colorful Model UC was built in 1935.

for further research. On the automotive scene however, progress continued apace on pneumatic tires. The emerging aircraft industry also needed larger and heavier tires, and these demands prompted the relatively young tire industry to further research and development. In 1932 Firestone Tire & Rubber Company built some specially designed tires for Allis-Chalmers, and the latter introduced them on their tractors later that year. In so doing, Allis-Chalmers made tractor history by being the first company to offer pneumatic tires as an option. Chalmers capitalized on their tractor tire developments by staging "tractor races" at various fairs in the early 1930s. Specially geared Model U tractors were used. Barney Oldfield, the famous racing driver, drove a Model U at a record speed of 64.33 mph on September 17, 1933.

With the introduction of pneumatic tires, much of the tractor industry, as well as many farmers, remained skeptical. Again, the Nebraska Tractor Tests were beneficial. Impartial testing manifested better fuel economy and more efficient delivery of power to the drawbar with rubber tires than with conventional steel wheels. These money-saving positives were further accentuated with vastly improved operator comfort achieved through the use of rubber tires.

Obtaining the proper type and size of tire was somewhat of a problem during the 1930s. In addition, a great many different lug styles were available, and some were far better than others. Yet, this new and exciting phase of tractor design evolved just as surely as the previous improvements on engines and drive trains. Tire manufacturers also discovered that adding water ballast to tractor tires greatly improved traction. Commercial calcium chloride was found to be a cheap and effective method of preventing freezing of the water, and inventors soon found a simple method of injecting water into the tire tube directly through the valve stem.

Some farmers continued to insist on steel wheels, and thus the rubber tires came as optional equipment on virtually all tractors up to 1940. With the onset of World War II, there were few new tractors built, and most of these were furnished with steel wheels, due to the scarcity of rubber tires. After World War II, very few tractors were available with steel wheels, as pneumatic tires became the norm.

Up to this point, the crawler tractor had gained only slight attention. Holt had built a few large crawlers at the turn of the century, and a few others, such as the Bullock, appeared about 1910. The picture changed dramatically when Cleveland Tractor Com-

BELOW:
A Caterpillar crawler tractor works a Philippine ricefield in 1931.

RIGHT:
Oliver Hart-Parr's Model 70, introduced in 1935, represented a marriage of form and function. The Model 70 featured a six-cylinder engine and a stylish, streamlined design.

pany introduced the first of their Cletrac models in 1916. Cletrac became quite popular, particularly since it could be furnished with a number of mounted implements.

During 1925 the C. L. Best Tractor Company and the Holt Mfg. Company merged to form Caterpillar Tractor Company. While the Caterpillar tractors were largely aimed for the construction industry, a great many were used for agricultural purposes. Another significant crawler was the Monarch, built at Springfield, Illinois. This firm was eventually bought out by Allis-Chalmers. Cletrac came into the ownership of Oliver Corporation. In the 1930s, the crawler tractor gained steadily in popularity.

Also of interest, the first imported tractors came onto the U.S. market in 1929. These were the "Irish Fordsons" built at the Ford factories in Ireland. They were much improved over the domestic version which had left the market a year before. The Irish Fordson had more power, used a high-tension magneto, and included water pump circulation.

BELOW:
The Massey-Harris entry into the row-crop tractor market was their 4WD General Purpose, introduced in 1931. The four-wheel-drive design featured equal-sized wheels in front and back.

Oliver Farm Equipment Company was formed in 1929. It was a merger of Oliver Chilled Plow Works, Hart-Parr Company, American Seeding Machine Company, and Nichols & Shepard Company. Within a year Oliver began introducing new tractor designs of the most modern styles.

Minneapolis-Moline Power Implement Company was also formed in 1929. This was a merger of the Minneapolis Steel & Machinery Company, Minneapolis Threshing Machine Company and the Moline Plow Company. Also of significance was the United Tractor & Equipment Corporation of Chicago, Illinois. It was organized by 32 independent manufacturers and distributors of tractors and implements. Plans called for a full line of United farm and industrial equipment. Allis-Chalmers, a member of the organization, built the tractor; it was sold as the United, and also by A-C as their Model U.

In 1930 general purpose row-crop tractors were being offered by International Harvester as their Farmall, by Oliver Farm Equipment as their Row-Crop, by Massey-Harris as their 4WD General Purpose, by Minneapolis-Moline as the K-T (Kombination Tractor), by J. I. Case as their Model CC, by John Deere as their GP, and by Allis-Chalmers as their All-Crop. The

Rumely 6 came onto the field that year, as did the Eagle Model 6A tractor.

During the 1930s, the IHC Farmall was the row-crop design to copy. It was the first commercially successful row-crop style, and there were few other options. Deere & Company however, had introduced their Model GP (10-20) tractor in 1928, and continued it in production until 1935. Its arched front axle permitted it to straddle low-growing crops, and Deere built a number of three-row implements especially for use with this model.

Another option of the early 1930s was the Rumely DoAll. This was essentially a convertible tractor. For ordinary field work, the DoAll looked like any other conventional four-wheel tractor. However, for cultivating, the front wheels and axle were removed, the rear wheels were shifted to a different position, and the cultivator was mounted integrally with the tractor. This design never saw more than a small modicum of success, nor did the three-row concept of the Deere. However, the John Deere GP was the first tractor to use a mechanical power lift

ABOVE:
The John Deere General Purpose Model B works a cornfield in 1935. Advertised to do the daily work of six to eight horses on a small farm, the two-cylinder tractor used less fuel than the larger and more powerful Model A.

LEFT:
Stationary harvesting in 1939, man, horse and the Allis-Chalmers 40 All-Crop and B tractor combine forces.

ABOVE:
International Harvester introduced its four-cylinder Farmall F30 in 1930. This F30 was built in 1937.

BELOW:
The stylishly streamlined 1938 Graham-Bradley, rated at 32 hp, was sold by Sears & Roebuck.

attachment, and most other companies followed suit within a short time.

For farmers and tractor builders alike, 1931 was a bad year. The Great Depression had taken hold, and total domestic tractor production for the year was only about 71,000 units, compared to over 200,000 a year earlier. However, International Harvester introduced their F-30 Farmall that year, and the Huber Mfg. Company at Marion, Ohio, announced two new general-purpose models. As previously indicated, tractor engines continued developing, year by year. Of particular importance, some Huber tractors of the period were equipped with the famous Ricardo head developed in England, and used otherwise on high performance engines. Without a doubt, the tractor industry was learning from the automobile and truck industries.

Sears & Roebuck, the famous mail-order house, entered the tractor market in 1931 with their Bradley two-plow tractor. It used a Waukesha engine and was built up from stock parts. Several other companies of the period built tractors under a similar plan. Of additional importance for 1931, Deere & Company entered the field with their first row-crop model. Caterpillar Tractor Company announced the first diesel-powered crawler tractor in 1931.

Tractor sales became even worse in 1932 when total production came to less than 19,000 units. For companies stretched to their financial limit, the Great Depression spelled their doom. However, Minneapolis-Moline intro-

duced their Universal tractor that year, and it became the first of an entire line of M-M row-crop tractors to follow. International Harvester Company announced their F-12 tractor in 1932, but the substantially built Lauson tractor, produced by John Lauson Company, left the market, along with numerous others.

Of long lasting importance was the Tocco process for hardening crankshafts. Developed by the Ohio Crankshaft Company of Cleveland, this process greatly strengthened the crankshaft, vastly extending its operating life. The Tocco process had already been adopted by several companies in 1932, and was eventually used by many others.

Cleveland Tractor Company introduced their first diesel-powered crawler in 1933. Although tractor production was better than in 1932, there were now only about 20 firms in the tractor business and 90 percent of the total production came from nine companies. These were: International Harvester, Deere & Company, J. I. Case, Massey-Harris, Oliver Farm Equipment, Minneapolis-Moline, Allis-Chalmers, Cletrac, and Caterpillar. All of these companies resulted from mergers or had acquired various lines over the years to broaden their overall operations. Eventually, several of these firms would merge again as the industry continued to evolve.

During 1934 the diesel engine made further progress in the farm tractor industry. However, most of these efforts were confined to large crawlers. At this point diesel engines were very expensive to build, and were economically feasible for applications running no less than a thousand hours per year. Yet, the experiments continued and Caterpillar continued building its diesel model. Meanwhile, Allis-Chalmers was continuing with their own diesel engine experiments and soon would introduce their own version. The Cletrac "35" Diesel appeared in 1934, as did the Bates "35" Diesel.

Sales of wheel tractors improved slightly in 1934, but remained very sluggish due to the Great Depression. However, John Deere introduced their famous Model A tractor in 1934. It was capable of burning distillate fuel, a fuel probably best described as being somewhat better than kerosene, but with somewhat less energy than gasoline. Distillate remained fairly popular until about 1950. However, it had some of the same problems as kerosene, in that it would not vaporize as well as

TOP:
Introduced in 1934, the John Deere General Purpose Model A was a row-crop tractor designed for the average size farm.

ABOVE:
International's TracTracTor T35 crawler featured a diesel engine.

ABOVE:
John Deere's Model D added depth to the company's line in the mid-thirties, which also included models A, B and GP.

gasoline. The best that could be done was to atomize it as much as possible. Consequently, a small quantity of unburned fuel remained in the cylinders, went past the rings, and ended up in the crankcase. The resulting "crankcase dilution" was a problem for which no easy solution was found.

Starting an engine on distillate was difficult, if not impossible, especially in cold weather. Consequently, there was the added effort of starting on gasoline and switching over to distillate after the engine warmed up. These and other problems caused many farmers to opt for gasoline as the fuel of choice.

By 1935 tractor sales had improved considerably. The row-crop tractor was now firmly entrenched as a tractor of choice, and rubber tires were quickly becoming the rule rather than the exception. Several tractors were now equipped with a mechanically operated "power lift" system. J. I. Case introduced their new "motor lift" system activated by a simple trip button on the operator's platform. Case also introduced a number of implements designed especially for use with their Model CC tractor and the "motor lift" system.

A notable development for 1935 was the Minneapolis-Moline Universal Model J Tractor. It featured a unique engine with an F-head valve arrangement. The intake valves were located in the head, and the exhaust valves were situated in the engine block. Minneapolis-Moline claimed that this provided maximum cooling for all the valves, and the exhaust valves gained additional cooling due to their location lower in the engine block. The Minneapolis-Moline Model MTA came out in 1935, and it could be furnished with a high compression head for use with 70 octane gasoline. It could also be furnished with a special road gear offering a top speed of 10 mph.

John Deere Tractor Company announced its Model B tractor in 1935 to accompany the large Model A row-crop style already on the market. In addition, Deere was also building other models, including the Model D and Model GP tractors.

Oliver Corporation introduced their Model 70 tractor in 1935; it was an evolvement of the 18-27 Row-Crop design. The Oliver 70 featured a smooth running six-cylinder engine. Oliver pioneered the use of the high compression engine in farm tractors. Gradually the entire industry would abandon the slow-speed, long-stroke designs with a relatively low compression ratio to a square bore and stroke, and eventually would come to oversquare designs.

International Harvester Company made tractor history with their 1935 introduction of the WD-40 Diesel. This was the first farm wheel tractor to be marketed with a diesel engine. It

BELOW:
The 1938 Oliver 70 featured a high-compression engine rated at 23-28 hp.

featured a unique starting system in which the engine was equipped with a carburetor and magneto. After a preset warmup time the engine automatically switched over to full diesel operation.

Caterpillar Tractor Company was moving ahead with its diesel engine line, and in 1935 the company announced three new diesel models. That same year, Caterpillar passed the milestone of building 10,000 diesel engines.

In March 1936 the first Co-op tractor was built. Duplex Machine Company at Battle Creek, Michigan, was the manufacturer, and the Co-op was sold through several distributors. Chief among these was the Farmers Union Central Exchange at St. Paul, Minnesota. The Co-op was never a sales threat to the major builders, but it was a high quality tractor with several interesting features.

Since the Co-op was built largely from stock parts, repairs were relatively easy. For instance, the transmission, axles and differential were built

by Clark Equipment Company. A six-cylinder engine was used, and this contributed to exceptional running smoothness. Another six-cylinder tractor emerging in 1936 was the Eagle 6-B. It was of the tricycle type with adjustable rear wheel width.

J. I. Case introduced their Model RC tractor in 1936, and Massey-Harris

TOP:
Caterpillar's small D2 tractor sold for $1,725.

ABOVE:
Built by Duplex Machine Company, the Co-op was a high-quality tractor sold through several distributors.

RIGHT:
Introduced in 1936, the Massey-Harris Challenger was rated at 16-27 horsepower.

began offering their famous Challenger design. The John Deere Model G first appeared in 1936. It was built along the same general lines as the other Deere row-crop models, but had more horsepower.

Streamlined hoods and grilles predominated the changes in farm tractor design during the late 1930s. Minneapolis-Moline was a leader in streamlined designs, as was Oliver. Allis-Chalmers went over to streamlining in 1938, as did John Deere. Minneapolis-Moline carried the concept a dramatic

ABOVE:
J.I. Case's Model RC, first built in 1936, was an 18 hp row-crop tractor with a Waukesha four-cylinder engine.

RIGHT:
Minneapolis-Moline's 1938 UDLX tractor, with a fully enclosed cab, was an idea ahead of its time. Only 125 of these streamlined tractors were built.

OPPOSITE BOTTOM:
The J.I. Case Model DC with an H cultivator.

step forward to their 1938 introduction of the UDLX tractor. It was completely hooded, included an enclosed cab, and sported full fenders on all wheels. Only about 125 of these tractors were built; farmers simply weren't ready to accept the added cost of what now wouldn't even be considered as minimum equipment. It would be another four decades before a fully enclosed and heated tractor cab would gain wide acceptance.

Closing out the 1930s was the Farmall F-14, a slightly more powerful version of the earlier F-12. IH had enhanced the appearance of its tractors in 1936 by replacing the drab gray of the past with a bright red finish. It didn't make the tractors run any better, but it certainly made them more attractive.

J. I. Case Company introduced their "D-Series" tractors in 1939. Their Model DC was a row-crop model and was commonly rated as a "three-plow" tractor. It featured adjustable rear wheel spacing, synchronized steering, belt pulley, pto shaft, and a power lift system. The newly styled hood was sold under the concept of "Eagle Eye Visibility" and this referred to the open design that permitted a much better view for the operator.

The Allis-Chalmers Model C was a small model of a tricycle design, and Oliver introduced their Row-Crop 60 model that weighed only 2,000 pounds. However, it was still capable of over 18 belt horsepower.

TOP:
Ford introduced the 9N, a small utility tractor, in 1939.

ABOVE:
The Ferguson three-point hitch system.

ABOVE:
Harry Ferguson (left) and Henry Ford discuss the Ferguson System on June 29, 1939, at the introduction of the Ford 9N tractor. The three-point hitch system, available on a mass-produced tractor for the first time, contributed greatly to the success of the 9N, which sold 300,000 units over the next eight years.

Minneapolis-Moline pioneered the use of LP-gas as a tractor fuel. Beginning in the late 1930s, M-M began experiments which ultimately led to a series of tractors using this fuel. During the 1940-1960 period LP-gas gained some popularity, but by the 1960s, the diesel engine was emerging as the power source of choice; it would eventually come to a predominant position as an economical and reliable prime mover.

The newly developed pto output shaft and the power lift system varied greatly in design from one manufacturer to another. Drawbar size and height was not at all established. During the 1930s the American Society of Agricultural Engineers (ASAE) worked to develop industry standards. In 1939 the ASAE issued standard specifications for the master power take-off shield, and the pto shaft and its relationship to drawbar height, for all agricultural tractors. Oliver followed the industry standard immediately, and other manufacturers adopted the standards eventually. Other ASAE standards for 1939 included wide-base rear tractor tires for all agricultural models. Again, Oliver immediately adopted these standards.

One of the most significant developments of the 1930s came in late 1938. Harry Ferguson and Henry Ford completed their famous "handshake agreement" whereby Ford was given license to build tractors using the three-point hitch system developed by Ferguson. Beginning in June 1939, the first of the Ford 9N's hit the market. Although it was a small utility tractor, the 9N could be furnished with a variety of implements to fit the innova-

LEFT:
The 1938 Fordson All-Around would soon take a back seat to Ford's 9N.

BELOW:
The Allis-Chalmers Model IU from 1936 was available with solid rubber tires.

BOTTOM:
Weighing in at only 2,000 pounds, Oliver's Row-Crop 60 could deliver 18 belt horsepower.

tive three-point hitch system.

Since Ferguson's three-point system was protected by patents, competing manufacturers were forced to develop their own mounted implement lines. Thus emerged the Fast-Hitch, Quick-Hitch, Snap Coupler, Eagle Hitch, and numerous other designs. Eventually the patents expired and the entire industry benefited from the three-point hitch.

Despite the Great Depression, during the 1930s the tractor industry evolved at a faster pace than ever before. Row-crop tractors became a practical reality, and rubber tires proved themselves, all the while relegating steel wheels to the salvage yards. Tractor engines were greatly improved; raising the compression, shortening the stroke, and increasing the rated speed all contributed to a reduction in size and weight, but still increased the horsepower output. Transmissions and power trains were greatly improved during the 1930s. By the end of the decade almost all models had at least four forward speeds, and a few had more. The three-point hitch was now a reality, and farmers had their first look at a tractor with a fully enclosed cab. Yet, as the 1930s came to an end, the farm tractor industry would soon find itself largely converted to building military equipment. World War II was on the horizon.

CHAPTER 5:
The 1940s

PAGES 66-67:
The Willys-Overland Universal Jeep.

BELOW:
IH's 1944 0-4 tractor.

BOTTOM:
IH's 1949 McCormick Standard W6.

THE TRACTOR INDUSTRY began the 1940s on a low note, with only 32 American tractor manufacturing companies, then struggled through the lean World War II years, to emerge into the post-war boom years. The enormous backlog of tractor orders and increasing need for tractors created a vast market after the war. The developmental work carried out during the war years could finally reach fruition when materials and manpower again became available, resulting in tremendous forward strides in tractor engineering, and many new tractor manufacturing companies offering many new improved models.

International Harvester Company began the decade of innovation by introducing two new tractors in 1940. These included the W-4, W-6 and W-9 tractors, all of standard-tread design. These were augmented with the O-4 and O-6 tractors, designed especially as Orchard tractors. Then there was the T-6, the crawler equivalent of the W-6. The diesel version of the T-6 was the TD-6, identified by adding "D". Also produced with gasoline or diesel engines were the W-6 or WD-6 standard-tread tractors, and the Farmall M or MD row-crop models. Included also in the Farmall M series were the T-9 and TD-9 crawler models.

In 1940 Caterpillar Tractor Company announced a new D-8 tractor with increased horsepower; its 128

horsepower yielded a maximum drawbar pull of over 26,000 pounds. Caterpillar also introduced its D-7 model with 80 brake horsepower from a four-cylinder diesel engine. Another Caterpillar offering was their new D-6 tractor, a model with a maximum pull of over eight tons and capable of nearly 70 belt horsepower, although it didn't technically reach the market until 1941.

Allis-Chalmers tested their new HD-7, HD-10, and HD-14 crawlers at Nebraska's Tractor Test Laboratory in October 1940. All of these tractors were equipped with two-cycle diesel engines built by General Motors. The HD-7 was rated at 45 drawbar horsepower, the HD-10 was rated at 65 drawbar horsepower, and this figure rose to fractions short of 100 horsepower for the HD-14. Allis-Chalmers also tested their Model C row-crop tractor in Nebraska in 1940. This model weighed only 3,200 pounds, used a tricycle design, and delivered about 22 horsepower.

John Deere Tractor Company con-

ABOVE:
A 1949 McCormick Farmall M makes time on the road. This three-plow, 34-39 hp row-crop tractor was also available in a high-crop version.

ABOVE:
Minneapolis-Moline's stylized RTU tractor.

ABOVE RIGHT:
The grille of the Massey-Harris 101 Super tractor.

BELOW:
The evolution of John Deere's "D" series (l to r): 1920s, 1930s, and 1953.

tinued production of their venerable Model D, but began offering a newly styled version with several improvements. In Nebraska Tractor Test No. 350 of 1940, the revamped Model D delivered nearly 31 rated drawbar horsepower. Deere also tested their two-cylinder Model B. This tractor weighed 3,900 pounds and was rated at about 17 drawbar horsepower. In 1940 John Deere introduced the new HN model; it was a derivation from the Model H introduced the year before.

Other companies were busy creating new tractor models in 1940 as well. The Massey-Harris 101 Junior tractor appeared. It featured a Continental four-cylinder engine, weighed 4,800 pounds, and was rated at 30.15 brake horsepower. J. I. Case sent their Model D and their Model VC tractors to the Nebraska Tractor Test Laboratory in 1940. The Model D was in the 30-35 brake horsepower class, while the

little Model VC had a maximum of 24 belt horsepower. Minneapolis-Moline tested their new RTU and ZTU tractors at Nebraska in 1940. Both were highly styled designs with their "Prairie Gold" finish and dark red wheels.

Tractor refinements continued into the following year. During 1941 J. I. Case Company introduced their new "S" series tractors. Smaller than the "D" series models, the Model S tractors were built in several styles to suit specific farming needs. The SC was the row-crop model. Meanwhile, the Huber Mfg. Company at Marion, Ohio, discontinued manufacturing farm tractors. Deere & Company introduced its small Model LA tractor; it was tested at Nebraska in June 1941 under No. 373. The Massey-Harris Model 81-R was tested in September of 1941, and their Model 101-R was the subject of the next test, No. 374. At the end of 1941 came the John Deere Model AR. It was a standard-tread version of the Model A row-crop which had entered the market several years earlier. This model closed out the 1941 testing year, and with the onset of war hostilities, all testing was suspended at the Nebraska Tractor Test Laboratory until 1946.

With America's involvement in World War II, an acute manpower shortage occurred almost immediately, so experimental work came to a virtual standstill on new tractor models. Many tractor factories were converted to war production. Worst of all, the vast majority of raw materials needed for tractor production were usurped by the war effort. Out of necessity, steel-backed bearings replaced bronze bearings in many instances. Steel and iron alloys made heavier use of molybdenum instead of the chromium that had formerly been used. Preventative maintenance was the rule rather than the exception. Due to the scarcity of repair parts, a great many tractors were repaired with used parts or locally machined replacements to keep them in service.

The scarcity of tractors, implements and parts did not end immediately with the end of hostilities in 1945. It

BELOW:
The Allis-Chalmers HD-11 crawler was diesel-powered. Like other tractor manufacturers of the time, Allis-Chalmers introduced innovative improvements and new models during the 1940s.

took a year or more to reconvert munitions plants back to tractor factories. By then there was a gigantic backlog of orders, and an unprecedented demand for tractors. There was also a large demand for tractors in Europe, especially because of the Marshall Plan, and consequently, export quotas were imposed to keep American farmers supplied with reliable power. In his book, *The Agricultural Tractor 1855-1950*, R. B. Gray notes that "as a result of this restriction, many new tractor companies sprang up overnight and offered their products for sale . . . and many tractors of inferior design and quality were turned loose in foreign countries."

Even though production was severely restricted, and new developments were nearly halted, Minneapolis-Moline had managed to release its new Model GTA tractor in 1942, and J. I. Case introduced the "V" Series tractors. Included in the latter were the VA, VAC, VAI, and VAO models. A casualty of the times was the well-known Keck-Gonnerman Company at Mt. Vernon, Indiana, which discontinued manufacturing tractors in 1942. Deere & Company introduced its Model GM tractor in 1943, and the Model A tractor saw first light from B. F. Avery & Sons of Louisville, Kentucky.

In 1944 Deere & Company introduced several modified styles of earlier models. Included was the HNH and HWH, ideal for use with sugar cane production; the BNH and BWH, along with the ANH and AWH, row-crop modifications of the model B and model A, respectively. All were high-clearance models.

International Harvester announced their OS-4 and OS-6 orchard tractors in 1945. These were simple modifications of the O-4 and O-6 tractors already in production. Two additional offerings from International Harvester were the WR-9 and WDR-9 tractors – special rice models in gasoline and diesel styles, respectively.

BELOW:
Minneapolis-Moline introduced the Model GTA tractor in 1942. A revamped version of the big Model G, the GTA was produced until 1947.

LEFT:
In the 1940s, John Deere presented new tractor series as well as new or modified models of old favorites.

LEFT:
A 1945 mock-up model of the Allis-Chalmers rear-engined Model G, which went into production in 1948. Rated 9.6-10.6 hp, the Model G was the company's smallest tractor to date.

BELOW:
Introduced in 1944, John Deere's BWH was a modification of the Model B.

BOTTOM:
Minneapolis-Moline introduced its UTC Cane tractor, derived from the Model U row-crop tractor, in 1945.

Willys-Overland Company at Toledo, Ohio, introduced its Universal Jeep for farm use in 1945. This model was a takeoff from the famous Army Jeep. However, it was altered by having a lower low speed gear, and a different transmission and rear axle ratio. The Universal Jeep could be furnished with a rear belt pulley and with a form of the three-point hitch. Also introduced in 1945 was the UTC Cane tractor from Minneapolis-Moline. It was essentially a modified form of the Model U row-crop tractor already in production.

Tractor testing resumed at Nebraska in July 1946. Ironically, the first tractor tested after World War II was not a conventional farm tractor but was the Ellinwood Bear Cat, a small garden tractor.

Several new tractor companies appeared in 1946. One was the Empire Tractor Corporation at Philadelphia, Pennsylvania. Their Model 88 was powered with a 40 horsepower Willys-Overland engine, and was fitted with a transmission transfer case like that used on the conventional Army Jeep. Empire followed a couple of years later with their Model 90 tractor. However, the entire operation folded by 1950.

Another interesting model was the Leader, from Leader Tractor Mfg. Company at Chagrin Falls, Ohio. This tractor featured a Hercules 35 horsepower engine, hydraulic lift and a pto shaft. Earthmaster Farm Equipment Company at Hollydale, California, introduced their Model C, 1-to-2 plow tractor. Earthmaster heavily advertised its Duomatic hydraulic control for virtually effortless handling of mounted or towed implements. B. F. Avery Company at Louisville, Kentucky, added the Model V tractor to its line. Eventually Avery models would be acquired by Minneapolis-Moline Company.

Toward the end of 1946 the oral agreement between Harry Ferguson and Henry Ford, began in 1938, came to an end. This resulted in the formation of Dearborn Motors Corporation at Birmingham, Michigan, which built the Ford tractors, while Harry Ferguson Inc. continued to market his Ferguson tractor. This little tractor be-

OPPOSITE TOP:
Leader Tractor Mfg. Company produced this four-cylinder Model D in 1948.

OPPOSITE BOTTOM:
The small and manageable Model V tractor, produced by B.F. Avery Company at Louisville, Kentucky.

LEFT:
Harry Ferguson poses on the first tractor to come off the line in his new tractor plant after his break with Henry Ford in 1948.

BELOW:
Cockshutt of Brantford, Ontario, featured the Model 40 on their catalog cover. The Model 40 was a larger, slightly later version of the 1940s' Model 30.

came very popular, virtually overnight. Through this model the concept of the small utility tractor gained a real foothold in the tractor industry.

Cockshutt Plow Company at Brantford, Ontario, introduced their new tractor line in 1947. It included the innovative, continuous-running independent power take-off. Oliver had introduced the concept in the 1930s, although it didn't gain large popularity at the time. In fact, the Hart-Parr tractors of the 1920s had been equipped with a live pto, although this was done out of mechanical necessity. Curiously though, the concept gained little attention until several years later.

Oliver Corporation continued to promote the concept of crawler tractors for row-crop duties. Their HG Cletrac was available in several tread widths to accommodate various farming practices. In addition, there were numerous row-crop implements available for this tractor model. The Oliver Cletrac was, of course, a continuation of the original Cletrac models developed by Rollin H. White. The Oliver

ABOVE:
The famous Model 44 row-crop style was one model in a new tractor series by Massey-Harris in 1947. Here a farmer mows mixed hay in Indiana.

RIGHT:
The Massey-Harris standard tread Model 55 was one of the most successful tractors in the company's new line.

Cletrac models continued to use the planetary steering system that White had developed in 1914.

Another notable entry into the 1947 market was the HD-19 crawler of Allis-Chalmers. This huge 20-ton tractor was equipped with a torque converter drive. It would be several years before other manufacturers would adopt this drive system to their tractors.

Massey-Harris came along with an entire new series of tractors in 1947. Included was the famous Model 44 row-crop style, along with the Model 55 standard-tread model.

International Harvester Company announced their Super A tractor, along with the little Farmall Cub. IH had been very active in the crawler tractor business, and in 1947 they introduced their TD-24 crawler. At the time, this was the largest crawler tractor ever built, having a capacity of 161 drawbar horsepower.

Postwar demand for new tractors surged to over 750,000 units in 1948. Of these about 40,000 were crawlers, nearly 530,000 were wheel-type farm tractors, and the remainder was walking and riding styles of garden tractors.

The Allis-Chalmers WD appeared in production quantities during 1948, and with it came the concept of spin-out rear wheel adjustment. Standard equipment included a live pto and live hydraulics.

Oliver came along with a new series of tractors: the 66, 77, and 88 models. These models were equipped with a live pto, and spark-fired engines were available in their kerosene-distillate (KD) style, or the high-compression gasoline (HC) models. In addition, Oliver offered diesel-powered versions.

Minneapolis-Moline Company was very active at this time, offering several new models in 1948. Included was the Model ZA with five forward speeds. This, and several other M-M models, could be configured in at least four different styles, although the ordinary tricycle design was the most popular.

A number of new tractor companies appeared in 1948, including the General Tractor Company at Seattle, Washington, which introduced its Westrac tractor at that time. Another was the Intercontinental Mfg. Company. Although it was well built, the Westrac model was on the market for only a short time. Jumbo Steel Products at Azusa, California, announced their Simpson Jumbo in 1948, and it, like several other new models, was of short duration.

Moving into 1949, many other small companies entered the field. Demand for tractors was insatiable at the time, so even rather poor designs were mod-

BELOW: An Oliver Super 77, equipped with a row-crop cultivator, in action.

ABOVE:
In 1949 the Dodge division of Chrysler Motors adapted their Power Wagon for tractor use.

RIGHT:
Ideas are shared and tractors compared at a county fair in Delaware. In the innovative 1940s, tractor manufacturers maintained active public relations to keep farmers informed of new developments in farm equipment.

erately salable. Unfortunately, a great many very good designs by small firms were not backed up with the nationwide advertising or extensive dealer network built up by the major companies.

Detroit Tractor Corporation at Detroit, Michigan, introduced a four-wheel, all-wheel-drive tractor in three separate sizes during 1949. Long Mfg. Company at Tarboro, North Carolina, entered the field with their Long tractor, and the National Farm Machinery Cooperative began selling their Co-op E-3 style. This was one of the first post-war tractors to feature a creeper gear as standard equipment. Fate-Root-Heath Company at Plymouth, Ohio, had previously announced their Silver King, and in 1949 they began production of a new and improved model.

Dodge Division of Chrysler Motors began offering their Power Wagon for tractor use; it was originally designed for use by the Armed Forces during World War II. Love Tractor Company at Eau Claire, Wisconsin, began production of a three-plow model powered by a Chrysler Industrial engine, and the Metal Parts Corporation at Racine, Wisconsin, announced their single-cylinder Haas Atomic tractor. Brockway Tractor Company at Chagrin Falls, Ohio, came out with four new models, and the Farmaster Corporation introduced two new tractors.

The 1949 offerings also included the Earthmaster Model D made at Hollydale, California, and the three-plow Friday tractor made at Hartford, Michigan. Gibson Tractor Company at Longmont, Colorado, began production on two new tractors. Unlike many of the other 1949 introductions, the Gibson would remain on the market for several years. Laughlin Tractor Company at Marshall, Texas,

announced their new Model C-27 tractor in 1949, and Custom Mfg. Company at Shelbyville, Indiana, came out with two new models.

The decade of the forties was truly a time of growth in the tractor industry. By 1942 the number of American tractor manufacturers had dropped to 32, but by 1949 the total number had risen to 141. In the next few years this figure would again fall dramatically, but for different reasons. As the 1940s came to an end, farmers were beginning to get their first look at entirely new tractors. The evolutionary process was continuing, and the 1950s would see changes far more dramatic than anything ever witnessed in the past.

CHAPTER 6: The 1950s

PAGES 80-81:
A farmer works his soybean field with an International Harvester 450.

BELOW:
John Deere's Model G delivered 35 horsepower. This high-clearance version was produced in 1953.

IN THE PERIOD UP TO 1950, operator comfort was not a great consideration. Following World War II, some tractor builders began incorporating comfortable seats, but few other conveniences were offered. In fact, the Minneapolis-Moline UDLX Comfortractor, with an enclosed cab, received a very poor reception after being introduced in 1938.

Tractor accidents happened far too often. Sometimes this was the result of mechanical failure of some kind, but more often than not, it was the result of unsafe practices and simple ignorance. During the 1940s a few efforts were made toward achieving greater tractor safety, including a safety switch that shut off the ignition if the operator left the seat. During the 1950s, tractor manufacturers would build new models with more regard for convenience and safety.

John Deere introduced its Model R tractor in 1949, with production coming into full bloom in 1950. This was the first diesel tractor built by Deere, and at the time it was the most powerful tractor built by Deere & Company. This diesel model was started by means of an auxiliary "pony" engine that operated on gasoline.

The decade of the 1950s saw the beginning of a horsepower race that would continue virtually unabated for the next 20 years. Oversized sleeves and pistons were a popular means of raising the power level, and high altitude pistons were used to raise the compression, thus increasing the horsepower. LP-gas and diesel fuel

LEFT:
Oliver's Super 99 Diesel, introduced in 1955, used a two-cycle GM engine.

BELOW:
Oliver's Super Series replaced the Fleetline Series in the 1950s. This Super 77, like the other Super models, was available with a gas or diesel engine.

TOP:
The Allis-Chalmers Model CA tractor.

ABOVE:
The 55 model was one of Massey-Harris's largest tractors in the 1950s.

both vied for a place in the market, providing the first real competition for the time-honored gasoline engine.

During the early 1950s Allis-Chalmers promoted their Traction Booster system, offering it initially on their Model CA tractor. In the 1940s Oliver had announced their Fleetline Series of tractors in three distinct models known as the 66, 77, and 88 tractors. After 1949 these models could be furnished with gasoline or diesel engines.

Massey-Harris announced their new tractor models shortly after World War II, with their 44 and 55 models being especially popular. The M-H 55 Diesel was one of this company's largest tractors, and in the 1950s market, it was one of the largest tractors built. A special advantage was the capability to operate hydraulic cylinders on towed implements.

During 1951 International Harvester introduced its Super C tractor. It was essentially the same as the Farmall C that preceded it, but with an increased power level. This was a harbinger of what would occur in the following years. Tractor models would undergo frequent increases in horsepower output. Sometimes this was achieved by raising the engine speed, and sometimes by raising the compression or increasing the cylinder diameter. In some instances, the in-

creased power levels caused premature engine bearing failures and transmission problems.

Minneapolis-Moline and B. F. Avery & Sons merged in 1951, with the small Avery tractor disappearing soon after. M-M also introduced its Model ZA tractor. This model had the same performance characteristics as the earlier Model Z but carried a slightly different appearance due to modified sheet metal. M-M also introduced its Model L Uni-Tractor in 1952. It was designed for use with several different machines, including the Uni-Combine, Uni-Baler, Uni-Husker, and Uni-Forager. Ten years later the entire Uni-line was sold to New Idea.

Changes abounded in 1952. Deere & Company introduced its first live pto system, and J. I. Case presented its latest version of the Model LA tractor. Case also featured the Eagle Hitch as an option on the Model D and Model S tractors. This design first appeared on the Model VAC of 1949.

International Harvester announced its "Super" series for the Farmall trac-

ABOVE:
In 1952 Minneapolis-Moline introduced its Uni-Tractor, which was designed for use with a range of implements, from the Uni-Combine to the Uni-Forager.

LEFT:
M-M's Uni-Tractor was powered by a V-type four-cylinder engine with a 3⅝″ × 5″ bore and stroke.

ABOVE:
A John Deere 420 at work. In 1956 Deere increased the power about 20 percent and added "20s" to the model designations of its tractors. The 420 was an upgrade of the 40.

tor line in 1952, and Minneapolis-Moline introduced its first diesel tractor in that same year. Behlen Mfg. Company at Columbus, Nebraska, introduced a power steering system that could be retrofitted to many different tractors. Before long, most manufacturers were offering integral power steering, at least as an option.

Massey-Harris and Ferguson Tractor merged in August 1953. Early the next year the new company took the name of Massey-Harris-Ferguson. Shortly after the name was shortened simply to Massey-Ferguson. Ford Motor Company announced its Model NAA tractor in 1953. Also called the Golden Jubilee, this model commemorated the 50-year anniversary of the founding of the Ford Motor Company.

J. I. Case announced its Model 500 diesel in 1953. This was the company's first six-cylinder tractor, as well as being its first diesel model. International Harvester introduced its "Fast-Hitch" system on the Super C, and later, on other models. At the time, the Ferguson three-point hitch was covered by patents, and competing manufacturers were forced to come up with their own designs that they hoped would not infringe on the Ferguson patents.

John Deere introduced its Model 70 tractor in 1953. It was available with engines that could operate on gasoline, distillate, propane, or diesel fuel. Deere also announced its 40 Standard and Tricycle models to replace the earlier M and MT tractors. The Wagner Bros. at Portland, Oregon, began building their four-wheel-drive tractor. Within a short time there were several competing companies in this field.

Another product of the times was the Oliver XO-121 experimental tractor. The XO-121 was a special engine design with a 12 to 1 compression ratio. It

LEFT:
John Deere's Model 70, introduced in 1953, was available with a gasoline, distillate, propane or diesel powered engine. This diesel version quickly gained favor. Beginning in 1954 power steering was also available.

BELOW:
A stepping stone between John Deere's Model M and 420, the 40 Standard featured a padded seat, independent rear brakes and handsome styling.

used a fuel with an octane rating of over 100. This amazing engine delivered nearly 45 percent more horsepower than the earlier Oliver 70. Although the XO-121 was never put into production, the test results had a profound effect on tractor engine design. However, the advantages would have a short life, since diesel engines would completely dominate the tractor market in a few more years.

International Harvester introduced its "TA" (Torque Amplifier) system in 1954. A hand lever connected to a planetary gear unit doubled the speed choices of the standard five-speed transmission. IH also introduced

ABOVE:
First introduced in 1949, John Deere's Model R was the company's first diesel tractor. A pony two-cylinder gas engine facilitated even cold-weather starting.

ABOVE:
John Deere's "30" series replaced the "20" series in 1958. The powerful 830 diesel replaced the 820.

their first live pto system in 1954. International Harvester Company announced its new Farmall 100, 300, and 400 tractors in 1955; the Farmall 200 had come onto the market the previous year. IH also introduced its International 300 Utility tractor. This low-profile design was the first of the IH utility tractor models, and most other tractor builders came out with utility tractor models during the 1950s.

J. I. Case came out with their 400 series tractors in 1955. They were available with gasoline, propane or diesel engines. An eight-speed transmission was a new feature, with power steering, independent pto, and the Case Eagle Hitch as options.

Ford Motor Company introduced five new tractor models in 1955. Prior to this time, Ford had built the 9N, 8N, and Ford NAA models, but in 1955 the company came out with row-crop models in addition to its established utility tractor line.

John Deere introduced the 80 Diesel as a replacement for the earlier Model R Diesel, and Oliver built its Super 99 Diesel. The latter used a two-cycle GM engine with a gear-driven scavenging blower. Minneapolis-Moline introduced the ZB tractor in 1955. It was an updated version of the earlier Model Z. M-M also announced their GB Diesel. This was their largest tractor and used the Lanova combustion system.

During 1956 Deere & Company introduced its 520, 620, and 720 tractor

ABOVE:
A John Deere 620 in action. In 1956 the 620 replaced the 60, which had in turn replaced the A tractor.

BELOW:
The six-cylinder Oliver 99 diesel was part of the Super Series introduced in 1954.

models. Included was the 720 Distillate style, and this was one of the last tractors to be built specifically for distillate fuel. Deere sent one of its 720 Diesels to the Nebraska Tractor Test Laboratory in 1956. In Test No. 594, the 720 Diesel came up with the amazing fuel economy of 16.56 horsepower hours per gallon of fuel. This record would stand for many years.

Massey-Harris-Ferguson continued building both the Massey-Harris and Ferguson tractor lines for a time. Integrating the two separate tractor lines required several years. As an example, the Massey-Harris 50 tractor was launched in 1956. This same tractor with some changes in sheet metal

and colors became the Massey-Ferguson 50 in 1958. Initially, the Massey-Harris 50 was also sold as the Ferguson 50. These two tractor models were the same except for the color and some external changes.

Minneapolis-Moline then introduced several new tractors in 1956, including the 445 and 335 models. Both were furnished with power steering and a three-point, draft-control hitch. The Ampli-Torc drive of M-M provided on-the-go power shifting, and this feature would soon be integrated within many other tractor models. Adjustable wide-front axles were becoming the rule rather than the exception by 1956. The concept had gained its first real impetus with the Ford 9N of 1939, but within two decades the adjustable wide-front axle was proving itself to be more safe than the tricycle front end. A few companies designed the adjustable wide-front so that in combination with power steering, the axles could be power-adjusted in only a few minutes' time.

J. I. Case acquired the American Tractor Company of Churubusco, Indiana, in 1957. America had been building crawlers since 1950, with the Terratrac line gaining considerable attention over the years. This acquisition put J. I. Case into the crawler tractor business with a thoroughly proven line, and was the forerunner of an ex-

OPPOSITE TOP:
This Massey-Harris 33 was powered by a gasoline engine. In 1956 the 33 was replaced by the updated 333.

OPPOSITE BOTTOM:
A John Deere 430 crawler works a field.

BELOW:
A worker prepares to demonstrate plowing with an Allis-Chalmers D-12 Series III tractor at the Allis-Chalmers sales farm in Racine, Wisconsin.

ABOVE:
An Indiana farmer rakes alfalfa with his Allis-Chalmers D-14 and a ground-driven rake. Introduced in 1957, the D-14 featured the innovation Power Director system.

tensive industrial equipment line from this manufacturer.

Steiger Mfg. Company was organized in 1957 to build a four-wheel-drive tractor. Their first model had an unprecedented 238 horsepower engine. Within a short time the Steiger tractors were being built in several models, and with ever-increasing power levels. A salient feature of the Steiger line was their Swinging Power Divider. This design reduced the angle of the drive line when turning, and improved turning ability.

J. I. Case introduced its Case-O-Matic drive in 1957. This revolutionary new concept included a torque converter ahead of an ordinary transmission. The torque converter could be locked out at will after gaining the desired operating speeds. On heavy pulls, the converter could be re-engaged with a hand lever or a foot pedal.

Allis-Chalmers announced their Power Director system on the new D-14 tractor of 1957. With the Power Director, ground speed could be reduced on-the-go for greater pulling

ability. The Oliver Super 99 Diesel appeared in 1957, and the Oliver Super 44 Utility model also came out that year.

During the late 1950s, several major changes were occurring in the tractor industry. External styling was becoming more important, and operator comfort was gaining extra attention. Upholstered seats had now replaced the pressed steel seat of earlier years almost exclusively. Diesel engines were gaining in popularity every year. The unquestioned economy of the diesel engine was a positive factor. However, until the 1950s, cold weather starting of the diesel was considered to be a problem. Improved fuel systems and the introduction of direct-injection diesels minimized many of these problems and made the diesel far more attractive, even in cold weather regions. Transmission designs were improving rapidly, with the torque converter system of the Case-O-Matic drive, and various methods of on-the-go shifting that came into prominence at this time. All of these positive developments would lead to even more refinement and improvement of virtually all tractor components.

ABOVE:
A striking design distinguished Minneapolis-Moline's 1956 335 model, which featured power steering, a three-point hitch, and Ampli-Torc drive. The four-cylinder engine delivered about 35 belt hp.

BELOW:
The Allis-Chalmers 1956 WD-45 was the first tractor with factory-installed power steering. A six-cylinder 230-ci diesel engine powered the WD-45.

ABOVE:
The McCormick Farmall 450 was introduced in 1956 as an upgrade of the 400. A white grille and hood slashes added contrast to the color scheme.

During 1959 the American Society of Agricultural Engineers (ASAE) developed a standard for the three-point hitch system. This move provided uniformity within the industry, and would prove to be a great benefit to farmers. With standardized hitch systems, implements made by one company could be readily used on a tractor of another make. The original three-point Ferguson system as employed on the Ford tractors would become known as the Category I hitch. In later years, bigger tractors and higher power levels necessitated larger hitch system components. Eventually then, the Category II and Category III hitches were developed. Since each category was built to ASAE standards, a farmer would be able to buy an implement of his choice and couple it to a tractor already on the farm. The same circumstances regarding drawbar and pto systems had troubled farmers and the industry some years earlier, but due to the ASAE standards, these components also came within general guidelines. As all of these various standards were developed, farmers were able to take full advantage of implements built by the full-line companies as well as the short-line manufacturers.

Tractor manufacturers were constantly looking for new and more efficient engine designs during the 1950s. For example, the Ford Typhoon tractor was developed in 1957. Although this model never got past the experimental stage, it broke new ground for tractor designers. The Typhoon was powered by a free piston turbine engine and included a power shift transmission in its design.

Allis-Chalmers introduced its fuel cell tractor in 1959. This experimental model was powered with over 1,000 individual fuel cells. These provided the electricity for driving the tractor. Allis-Chalmers had pioneered many of the concepts used in fuel cell designs, so this tractor was a natural evolvement of the previous research. This design had twice the efficiency of other tractors of its time, had no moving parts, and no exhaust. This significant example of tractor development is now housed in the Smithsonian Institution in Washington, D.C. Today a renewed interest in the "electric car" seems to portend that a refined version of the A-C fuel cell tractor might someday come off an assembly line.

By the late 1950s a few farm tractors were coming into the United States from other countries. This trend would grow in the following years, with many U.S. manufacturers opting to build certain tractor models in another country and import them into the United States. By the 1980s, few tractors of under 100 horsepower were being built in the United States, regardless of make. The majority were either completely built overseas, or at the least some of the components were manufactured in a foreign country and exported from there to a U.S. assembly plant.

The decade of the 1950s saw some of the most dramatic changes ever witnessed in the relatively young tractor manufacturing industry. Only 40 years earlier, tractors were large, unwieldy machines that were useful for only heavy belt or drawbar work. During the 1950s however, the farm tractor had evolved into a highly efficient workhorse, and designers were now looking at new ways to enhance operator comfort, along with new mechanical developments. The diesel engine was becoming firmly entrenched as the engine of choice, and in the decade of the 1960s it would predominate within the industry.

ABOVE:
Originally produced in 1945 by B.F. Avery & Company, this tractor was introduced by Minneapolis-Moline in 1951 as the Model BF after M-M took over Avery.

BELOW:
The Oliver Super 55, introduced in 1954, was rated at 30-34 hp.

CHAPTER 7:
The 1960s

PAGES 96-97:
The John Deere 4010 diesel in action.

BELOW:
John Deere's "New Generation" 1010 Series.

BOTTOM:
John Deere's 3010 row-crop diesel operates a 406 lister planter.

JOHN DEERE TRACTOR Company made history in 1960 by closing out its time-honored line of two-cylinder tractors. For several decades, Deere had been the only remaining manufacturer using a two-cylinder engine. However, the demand for increased power levels simply pushed this style beyond its practical limits. Although two-cylinder engines could be built with a larger output, the engine itself became too wide for practical row-crop use.

The in-line gear train used in the two-cylinder models was the ultimate in simplicity, and the 720 Diesel model had set a record in fuel economy. Yet, the days of the two-cylinder, cross-mounted engine finally came to an end.

John Deere went to work on an entirely new design, coming out with its "New Generation" tractors in 1960. Initially, the new line included the 1010, 2010, 3010, and 4010 tractors. Of these, the latter three were available in gasoline, propane and diesel versions. The 4010 used a six-cylinder engine, while the three smaller sizes were built with a four-cylinder design.

Features abounded in the New Generation John Deere tractors. The 3010 and 4010 were furnished with power brakes as standard equipment, and power steering was standard on all models. Hydrostatic power steering was standard on the 3010 and 4010 models. This eliminated any mechanical link between the steering wheel and the front wheels of the tractor.

International Harvester Company launched some major new designs for its 404 and 504 tractors in 1960. Included was this company's first U.S.-

TOP:
A farmer works a field with a John Deere 2010 diesel, part of Deere's "New Generation" tractors introduced in 1960.

LEFT:
Powered by a six-cylinder engine, John Deere's 4010 featured power brakes and hydrostatic power steering. The 4010 was available in gasoline, diesel or propane versions.

ABOVE:
The J.I. Case 830 model works a cornfield. Introduced in 1960, the "30" series included the 730 and 830 models, which could be equipped with the Case-O-Matic torque converter drive or a standard eight-speed transmission.

designed three-point hitch system with a hydraulic draft control. A torsion bar was used for draft sensing on the top link, and this design was an industry first with International Harvester.

The Farmall and International Harvester 404 and 504 tractors for 1960 were also equipped with an oil cooler for the transmission and hydraulic systems. Increasing loads imposed on these components necessitated this equipment.

Dry air cleaners, which were gaining wide acceptance, were introduced by IH on the 404 and 504 models. Hydrostatic power steering was also featured on the 404 and 504 IH tractors, and this too, was indicative of the tremendous changes taking place in farm tractor design.

Oliver Corporation was actively promoting its 1800 and 1900 tractor models. These would see several different versions going into the 1960s. The Oliver 1800 was built in an anniversary model commemorating the company's quarter-century mark in manufacturing six-cylinder tractor engines. When the first Oliver 70 with a six-cylinder engine appeared during the 1930s, numerous farmers and industry watchers thought that this design "was too much like a car engine" and it would never hold up in the field. However, the Oliver six-cylinder engines proved themselves over and over in the following years, with many other companies eventually adopting the six-cylinder design. Oliver Corporation was acquired by White Motor Company in 1960 as a wholly owned subsidiary. Eventually the Oliver line disappeared as a distinct entity, being replaced with a series of White farm tractors.

J. I. Case Company introduced a new series of farm tractors in 1960. Included were the 430, 530, 630, 730,830 and 930 models. The 730 and

830 models could be equipped with either the Case-O-Matic torque converter drive or with a standard eight-speed transmission. Case also offered their big 930 tractor with the option of a standard 540 rpm pto shaft or with a 1,000 rpm pto.

Turbochargers became more and more evident in tractor designs of the 1960s. When Allis-Chalmers introduced its D-19 turbocharged diesel in 1961, it caught the attention of the entire industry. Allis-Chalmers had previously been building turbocharged industrial engines at the Harvey (Illinois) Works and had considerable experience in this field. Previously, the Harvey Works was the Buda Engine Company. The latter had been building engines since early in the century, and during the 1930s was offering the Buda-Lanova engines in many sizes and styles. This expertise led to the Buda-designed diesels with gear-driven, positive displacement turbochargers on numerous models. Many of these had been used by the military during World War II.

International Harvester Company made history with their 1960 unveil-

ABOVE:
Spring plowing with the Oliver 1800, a model which would appear in many different versions in the 1960s.

LEFT:
Case introduced their big 930 tractor in 1960.

ing of the HT-340 experimental gas turbine tractor. Although the gas turbine of the HT-340 weighed but 60 pounds, it had a maximum operating speed of 57,000 rpm. After suitable reduction gearing, the turbine operated a hydraulic pump. It in turn powered a hydraulic motor which operated the tractor. Even though the HT-340 was never marketed, the concept of a hydrostatic drive developed in this model would later be used in several IH tractors. The HT-340 is now in the Smithsonian Institution.

International Harvester also introduced its Model 4300 four-wheel-drive tractor to the market in 1961. This was the largest and most powerful tractor of its time, being capable of over 300 horsepower. The engine was a six-cylinder, 817 cubic inch, turbocharged diesel.

During 1962 White Motor Company acquired Cockshutt Farm Machinery Ltd. of Canada. White had previously acquired Oliver Corporation, and in 1963 the company bought the Minneapolis-Moline line. At the end of the 1960s, 1969 to be exact, White merged all of its interests into White Farm Equipment, and the latter became a wholly owned subsidiary of White Motors Corporation. At this point, Oliver, Cockshutt, and Minneapolis-Moline tractors faded from the scene as distinct entities and were replaced with an entirely new series of White farm tractors.

John Deere introduced its 5010 Diesel in 1962, and this was the company's first tractor with more than 100 horsepower. Allis-Chalmers countered in 1963 with their announcement of the big D-21. The latter model incorporated many new features for Allis-Chalmers, including hydrostatic power steering and a 1,000 rpm pto shaft.

International Harvester came into the 1963 market with the 706 and 806 Series tractors. These models had completely new drive train and hydraulic systems, designed to satisfy the demands of farmers and to counter the inadequacy of older systems to withstand increased power levels. The new

ABOVE:
A farmer turns the soil with the big Allis-Chalmers D-21. Introduced in 1963, the D-21 featured hydrostatic power steering and a 1,000 rpm pto shaft.

LEFT:
An Allis-Chalmers D-21, with an enclosed cab, combines power and modern amenities.

OPPOSITE TOP:
This diesel-powered Case 430 was a versatile component of the 1960 "30" series.

OPPOSITE BOTTOM:
Farmers collect and bale hay with a John Deere 3020 on steel wheels.

ABOVE:
The Oliver 1950 was part of the company's "50" series, introduced in 1964 and offering such new features as Hydra-Letric hydraulics and a tilt-telescope steering wheel.

transmission was in tandem with a two-speed range shifter, and this provided eight forward speeds. When combined with the International Harvester Torque Amplifier system, a total of sixteen forward and eight reverse speeds were possible.

On the comfort side, the 706 and 806 tractors had the seat moved forward of the rear axle to provide a smoother ride and enhance operator comfort. Hydrostatic power steering was standard equipment, as was a power-shift dual-speed pto shaft. Transmission and hydraulic oil coolers were standard, and a factory-installed front-wheel-drive attachment was optionally available.

Oliver introduced its "50" Series tractors in 1964. Included were the 1250, 1550, 1650, 1750, 1850, and 1950 models. Oliver also announced its new "Certified Horsepower" policy. A label was attached to each tractor, attesting to its performance prior to leaving the factory. New features of this series included a tachometer, dry air cleaner, tilt-telescope steering wheel, Hydra-Lectric hydraulics, and a three-point hitch.

Ford Motor Company had been enlarging and expanding its line during the 1950s, and continued to broaden its sales and manufacturing bases by opening new plants in England and Belgium during 1964.

J. I. Case made history in 1964 with the introduction of their first four-wheel-drive tractor, the Model 1200 Traction King Diesel. With the Model 1200 Traction King, Case began using their newly designed 451-cubic-inch diesel engine. This particular engine would see extensive use in numerous

LEFT:
First announced in late 1962, Minneapolis-Moline's G706 was rated at 102 pto hp. One of the largest of the M-M line, the G706 was equipped with power assist front wheels and a five-speed gearbox.

BELOW:
Farmers auger grain from a combine into wagons. International Harvester's Farmall 706, introduced in 1963, was designed to meet the farmer's demands for power and comfort.

RIGHT:
Making the first cut of hay on an Iowa farm with a dependable Ford. Ford had been a one-tractor company until 1955, when the company expanded its line to five tractors.

BELOW:
A J.I. Case Model 1470 Traction King diesel discs a seedbed in preparation for planting. By the end of the decade Case had been purchased twice, the second time by Tenneco.

Case tractor models in the coming years.

In 1965 the first Japanese-built agricultural tractors appeared in the United States. The Kubota RV gasoline and the Kubota D-20 Diesel were announced by Kubota Iron & Machinery Works of Osaka, Japan. Thus began a change in the American tractor market which would swell considerably in the coming years.

International Harvester entered the 1965 market with their new models, the 1206, 4100, and 656 tractors. IH went over the 100 horsepower mark with their new 1206. It was equipped with Harvester's own six-cylinder, 361-cubic-inch turbocharged engine. IH also was a trendsetter in 1965 by offering a factory-installed cab with heating and air conditioning. Within a very short time, virtually every tractor builder offered heated and air conditioned tractor cabs as an option. With the introduction of the factory-installed cab came another dimension, that of sound engineering. Tractor engineers would immediately set to work at lowering the sound levels inside the cab, as well as otherwise improving the operating environment. At this time, tractor builders were also making new efforts at providing rollover protection with specially built guards and frames.

Deutz tractors from Germany made their first major entry into the U.S. market during 1966. The unique

ABOVE:
International Harvester's 656 tractor harvests hay into round bales. The 656 was one of IH's three new offerings in 1965.

OPPOSITE TOP:
A 1969 Allis-Chalmers 220 plows a field. Allis-Chalmers' tractor division enjoyed success and independence until the 1980s, when it would be sold.

OPPOSITE BOTTOM:
A Massey-Ferguson 1135 works a field. This formidable tractor was as comfortable as it was large.

Deutz air-cooled diesel was well received, and quickly gained a reputation for economy and reliability.

Massey-Ferguson came into the 1966 market with their Model 1130 Diesel. This big tractor carried a 354-cubic-inch engine and was the first M-F tractor to use a turbocharger.

As previously noted, International Harvester unveiled its experimental HT-340 gas turbine tractor in 1961. This design used a hydrostatic transmission. Now in 1967, Harvester announced the 656, the company's first tractor with hydrostatic drive. The 656 Hydro used a piston-type hydraulic pump which furnished hydraulic power to a piston-type hydraulic motor. A single lever controlled the movement of the tractor, and because of the hydrostatic design, ground speed was infinitely variable, at the will of the operator.

As the 1960s came to a close, the race for increasing horsepower continued. Several companies, such as Versatile and Steiger, built four-wheel-drive tractors exclusively. Most of the major farm equipment companies included four-wheel-drive models as part of their total offering. Turbocharged diesel engines were now commonplace. The increased power levels necessitated engine features such as oil-cooled pistons and oil cooling for the crankcase. Hydraulic brakes were now the industry norm, and many larger tractors used power braking.

Engine designs continued to change. Gasoline engines were fast approaching their end, and propane had virtually disappeared from the scene. The diesel engine was quickly becoming the engine of choice. Although the Lanova and other time-honored designs were efficient and economical, new engine designs had been making inroads. Of significance was the Roosa Master injection pump and the introduction of the Roosa-designed pencil injectors. During 1969 J. I. Case replaced the Lanova system with its precombustion cells with an innovative new open chamber system

BELOW:
A versatile 935 prepares a seedbed and applies anhydrous. Versatile was a major player in the 1960s' race for increasing horsepower.

of the direct-injection type.

With the close of the 1960s, the evolutionary process of tractor development had slowed somewhat over the previous decades. To be sure, tractor developments continued unabated. However, these developments were often of new features such as enclosed cabs or comfortable seating rather than of developing an entirely new chassis design like the Farmall Row-Crop of the 1920s. The emphasis was now on such practical matters as increasing horsepower, comfort, safety, operating economy and reliability. Tractor engineers applied their talents to these problems and have continued to develop farm tractors of unprecedented quality.

CHAPTER 8: 1970-present

PAGES 110-111:
A four-wheel-drive John Deere 8630 equipped with herbicide tanks and a field cultivator prepares a seedbed.

BELOW:
A Massey-Ferguson Model 1105 with a John Deere bailer. Massey-Ferguson struggled through the difficult 1980s but remained intact.

OPPOSITE:
Farmhands bail hay with an Allis-Chalmers Model 8030 and a John Deere bailer. In 1985 Allis-Chalmers was purchased by Klockner-Humboldt-Deutz and renamed the Deutz-Allis Corp.

DURING THE 1970s, increasing demands for large horsepower led to unprecedented production of two-wheel drive tractors in excess of 100 horsepower and four-wheel-drive models of even larger dimensions. Manufacturers concentrated much of their energy and resources on these big designs, and continued breaking new ground with better engines and drive trains. Beginning in 1970, Nebraska's Tractor Test Laboratory began conducting tests on the sound levels within tractor cabs. These tests were very beneficial in the design of new cabs with dramatically lower sound levels than anything ever marketed. Great emphasis was placed on cabs with comfortable seats, convenient console-mounted controls, and the addition of accessories such as radios and interior lighting.

Yet, trouble loomed on the horizon. A collapsing farm economy in the early 1980s forced many farmers into bankruptcy, while many others curtailed their buying of new equipment. History was repeating itself. In the early 1920s, a depressed farm economy and overproduction of tractors saw the disappearance of virtually hundreds of tractor and implement manufacturers of that time. Through mergers and perseverance, a substantial number of tractor companies remained in business up the the early 1930s. However, the Great Depression of that period finished off all but the strongest firms. When recovery finally came, World War II followed almost immediately, and this curtailed tractor production through most of the 1940s. A somewhat similar pattern would emerge in the late 1980s.

American agriculture was undergoing tremendous change. When the gasoline tractor saw first light less than a century ago, farming was very labor intensive. Something less than six decades later, a single person was able to efficiently farm more acres than a dozen men and several dozen horses could have farmed in the past. Already in the 1950s the horsepower race had

ALLIS-CHALMERS
8030

ABOVE:
Modern, large farms require large and powerful farm equipment. Here an Allis-Chalmers tractor in the 7000 series begins a day of spring planting.

RIGHT:
Spring corn planting in Iowa with an Allis-Chalmers Model 7020.

LEFT:
An International Harvester Model 766 round bailing with a Vermeer. In 1989 International Harvester succumbed to the times and sold the farm tractor and implement divisions to Tenneco, merging with Tenneco-owned Case.

BELOW:
An International Harvester 1056 brings in the cattle.

RIGHT:
An International Harvester 4786 works a cornfield with a 10-bottom plow.

BELOW:
A John Deere 4430 equipped with a pesticide tank works over a field. John Deere weathered the troubled 1970s and 1980s, when many farm equipment manufacturers went bankrupt or were bought out. The high casualty rate was due to overproduction, outdated factories, foreign competition, high interest rates and a failing farm economy.

begun. In some instances, the horsepower output of a tractor seemed more important than its fuel economy and its ability to perform day after day without service problems. By the 1980s it was obvious that there was far more tractor production capability than there was a market to buy the new units coming off the assembly line.

Part of the problem with excessive manufacturing capacity went back to the postwar period. At that time there was an insatiable need for new farm tractors. Many farmers who had been unable to afford a new tractor during the Great Depression were frustrated in their attempts to get a new one for the duration of World War II. After the war ended in 1945 there were a great many tractors in the field with an age of 20 or more years. Tractor builders responded with a flood of new tractors to meet the need, and many added to their production facilities for the purpose. Once built, the new factories remained in production, and slowly but surely contributed to the excessive

production that would follow. Complicating the problem still further was the fact that many tractor production plants were geared to smaller two- and three-plow tractors. There simply wasn't the space to build the 100-plus horsepower tractors in demand by the 1970s.

Too much production capability, obsolescent production facilities, and market saturation were some of the factors contributing to the decline and fall of the tractor empire during the 1970s and 1980s. Foreign competition added a further complication, and the

failed farm economy of the 1980s was another mitigating factor. The result was that many tractor manufacturers either disappeared from the scene through outright bankruptcy or lost their identity through mergers and buyouts. The shakeout that followed had a profound effect throughout all agricultural areas of the United States. Many small towns had an agricultural equipment dealership as one of their last drawing cards. In many instances, a manufacturer quit business, leaving the dealer without a tractor line, and consequently without a business. During the 1970s and 1980s, farm equipment dealers left the business in droves. Through these troubled times in the farm tractor business, only the strongest survived. Despite the traumatic times, the industry survived, and eventually revived itself to become even stronger than before.

In its infancy, the tractor industry depended largely on itself for the needed components. By the 1920s a few tractors were built from component parts, and this practice continued

ABOVE:
The four-wheel-drive Case 2470 Traction King plows a cornfield.

RIGHT:
A Case Model 1390 delivers a load of haybales.

ABOVE:
A Case Model 970 pulls a McCormick hay bailer.

into the early 1950s. As time went on, however, tractor builders became less hesitant to use components that might have been developed within another industry.

The automobile and truck industries provided much of the developmental work that eventually led to four- and six-cylinder engines that featured a shorter crank stroke and higher engine speeds. The truck industry in particular had developed transmissions and drive trains for heavy duty service, and many of these concepts were eventually borrowed by the tractor builders.

Diesel engines had their first application in purely stationary duties that included electric generator service. By the late 1920s a few engines had been developed suitable for tractor duty, but the early models were quite complicated and very heavy. The Lanova design was pioneered in the U.S. by a few companies, and in particular by the Buda Company at Harvey, Illinois. Buda developed diesels for the truck and marine industries, and many of these styles were later applied to farm tractor designs.

During World War II, hydraulics came into prominent use for military applications, and many of these developments were later applied to farm tractors. The fuel cell, as developed by Allis-Chalmers, found its first use in military and aerospace applications. Although the A-C fuel cell tractor never got past an experimental model, much of the technology was later applied to farm tractor design. Perhaps the day will come when this

DEUTZ-ALLIS
DEUTZ-ALLIS
9170
DEUTZ-ALLIS

ABOVE:
The Deutz-Allis lineup. In 1990, five years after Allis-Chalmers became Deutz-Allis, a group set up an American-based holding company, Allis Gleaner Co. (AGCO), and purchased the Deutz-Allis Corp.

LEFT:
A Deutz-Allis 9130 works a field.

OPPOSITE:
Ensconced in a Deutz-Allis 9170, a farmhand works through sunrise.

WHITE

pioneering work will result in a new kind of fuel cell tractor – one that hasn't yet been thought of.

The International Harvester gas turbine tractor was another experimental design that never got past a single copy, and it now resides in the Smithsonian Institution as a museum piece. However, this model included a hydrostatic transmission, and a few years later this concept was incorporated into several different International Harvester Hydro tractors.

A host of electrical and electronic devices have found their way into tractor design in recent years. Many of these devices provide the operator with unprecedented control and monitoring capabilities. There is no doubt that these trends will continue in coming years, restricted only by the pace of technological development.

Thus we see the evolutionary development of the Great American Farm tractor. Although largely unrecognized by the general populace, the American farm tractor has changed the face of American agriculture and America in general, in ways far beyond a perfunctory glance.

LEFT:
A White 4-150 discs a seedbed in preparation for planting. White Farm Equipment Company was purchased by Allied Farm Equipment Group in 1985. In 1991 White Tractor Division was bought by AGCO.

BELOW:
An AGCO Allis 9630, built to provide the power and efficiency required by today's farm conglomerates. The AGCO Allis division was formed when a U.S. management team bought Deutz-Allis and formed AGCO.

OPPOSITE:
A John Deere Model 4440 with a row-crop cultivator works an enormous cornfield. Established in the nineteenth century, John Deere is one of the few old-time tractor manufacturers to maintain its tradition of independence even to the present.

BELOW:
A John Deere Model 2755 at work after the harvest.

PAGE 126:
Spring planting in Iowa with a John Deere 4430.

Over a century ago, J. I. Case built its Paterson experimental tractor. It was no success, and was never marketed. In fact, another two decades would pass before Case would once again enter the tractor business. At the turn of the century, Hart-Parr Company launched the "gasoline traction engine," as it was then classified. Later, Hart-Parr would shorten the name simply to "tractor."

After 1913 the farm tractor industry evolved at a frenzied pace. Even though it took decades for some design features to emerge, from a historical perspective tractor development moved ahead at a surprisingly fast pace. The impact of the machine tool industry on tractor manufacturing is often overlooked. With the development of new machine tools and improved tooling, production of component parts was done with ever greater efficiency, and the quality of parts improved dramatically. Heat treating and other processes permitted components of greater strength, better durability, and less weight than ever before. Likewise, the role of metallurgy on tractor design is largely overlooked when considering the evolution of the farm tractor.

Today's farm tractor is the result of many different manufacturing processes, and these in turn are the result of untold hours spent in engineering and design. No longer is the Great American Farm Tractor an entity unto itself. It is the collective result of many different industrial developments, each of which plays a role in the overall product. The possibilities are endless, and the evolution of the American farm tractor is yet in its infancy.

4440
JOHN DEERE
RM

EERE
4430

Index

Numerals in *italics* indicate illustrations.

Picture Credits

AGCO Corporate Group: 120, 121(both), 123(bottom right).
J. C. Allen and Son, Inc.: 24-25, 27, 29(top), 32, 38(top), 40-41, 48(top), 52, 54, 57(top), 61(top), 66-67, 76(top), 80-81, 96-97, 101(top), 105(bottom), 106-107(bottom), 108, 109(bottom), 110-111, 116-117, 118(top), 122-123.
The Bettman Archive: 4-5, 8-9, 11(bottom), 12, 16, 20(top), 64, 75(top), 78-79(bottom).
John Cook/Iron Horse Power Magazine: 53(top, bottom), 65(top), 68(top).
Deere & Company Archives: 46(bottom), 47(bottom), 70(bottom), 87(bottom), 88(top), 98(both).
Heartland Images: 100, 118(bottom), 124(top).
Midwest Old Threshers Museum (photographs by Jim Adams and Sam Wynn): 6, 30(top), 33(bottom), 39(bottom), 44(bottom).
Andrew Morland: 1, 7(both), 17, 22, 29(bottom), 31(top), 33(top), 34(both), 35, 37(top), 39(top), 44(top), 45(both), 46(top), 47(top), 49(center, bottom), 53(center), 55(top), 56(bottom), 58(both), 59(top), 60(bottom), 61(bottom), 62(all three), 63(top, center), 65(bottom), 68(bottom), 69, 70(top left, top right), 72(top), 73(center, bottom), 74(both), 76(bottom), 82, 83(both), 85(both), 87(top), 89(bottom), 90(top), 93(both), 94, 95(both), 105(top).
Morning Star Photo: 2, 77, 78(top left), 102(bottom), 106(top), 107, 112, 113, 114(both), 115(both), 116(bottom), 119, 124(bottom), 125.
Ozark Stock: 18(top), 23.
Collection of C. H. Wendel: 10, 11(top), 13, 14, 15, 18(bottom), 19, 20(bottom), 21(both), 26, 28, 30(bottom), 31(bottom), 36, 37(bottom), 38(bottom), 42, 43(both), 48(bottom), 49(top), 50-51, 55(bottom), 56(top), 57(bottom), 59(bottom), 60(top), 63(bottom), 65(center), 70(bottom), 71, 72(bottom), 73(top), 75(bottom), 84(both), 86, 88(bottom), 89(top), 90(bottom), 91, 92-93, 99(both), 101(bottom), 102(top), 103(both), 104, 109(top).

Acknowledgments

The author and publisher would like to thank the following people who have helped in the preparation of this book: Barbara Thrasher, who edited it; Rita Longabucco, who did the picture research; Design 23, who designed it; and Elizabeth Miles Montgomery, who prepared the index.